IMAGES OF ASIA

Old Hanoi

Titles in the series

Old Hanoi

MARK SIDEL

For Gine –

With respect and

affection –

Mk

April '99

KUALA LUMPUR
OXFORD UNIVERSITY PRESS
OXFORD SINGAPORE NEW YORK
1998

Oxford University Press

Oxford New York

Athens Auckland Bangkok Bogotá Buenos Aires
Calcutta Cape Town Chennai Dar es Salaam Delhi
Florence Hong Kong Istanbul Karachi
Madrid Melbourne Mexico City Mumbai
Nairobi Paris São Paulo Shah Alam Singapore
Taipei Tokyo Toronto Warsaw

and associated companies in
Berlin Ibadan

Oxford is a trade mark of Oxford University Press

Published in the United States
by Oxford University Press, New York

© Oxford University Press 1998
First published 1998

British Library Cataloguing in Publication Data
Data available

Library of Congress Cataloging-in-Publication Data
Sidel, Mark.
Old Hanoi/Mark Sidel.
p. cm.—(Images of Asia)
Includes bibliographical references and index.
ISBN 983 56 0051 1 (hardcover)
1. Hanoi (Vietnam)—History. 2. Hanoi (Vietnam)—Description
and travel. I. Series.
DS559.93.H36S58 1998
959.7—dc21
98–20068
CIP

Typeset by Indah Photosetting Centre Sdn. Bhd., Malaysia
Printed by KHL Printing Co. (S) Pte. Ltd., Singapore
Published by Penerbit Fajar Bakti Sdn. Bhd. (008974-T)
under licence from Oxford University Press
4 Jalan U1/15, Seksyen U1, 40150 Shah Alam,
Selangor Darul Ehsan, Malaysia

Acknowledgements

THIS short work has many sponsors and friends, and it is a pleasure to acknowledge them here. I am grateful to Tim Karr who helped make arrangements for many of the photographs in this book, both from archives in Hanoi and those provided by his colleagues Nguyen Hong Sam and Nguyen Huy Kham. Geraldine and John Kunstadter provided financial support for travel and materials through the Albert Kunstadter Family Foundation, and I take this opportunity to express my gratitude for their generosity.

Susan Berresford, Barry Gaberman, Peter Geithner, and Mary Zurbuchen enabled me to work in and with Vietnam from 1992 to 1995 when I directed the Ford Foundation's programmes in that lovely and scarred nation. Sisamorn Plengsri, Sunanthana Kampanathsanyakorn, Pimpa Molkul, David Thomas, and Bill Klausner were kind and gracious colleagues and remain treasured friends. The dedicated and knowledgeable staff of the Americas Department of the Vietnamese Ministry of Foreign Affairs hosted my stays in Hanoi and are fine representatives of a renewed Vietnam. Huynh Mai Huong provided research assistance in Hanoi and Yu Hui helped with research in the United States.

My education about Vietnam, however incomplete, has incurred enormous debts to many. Without any possibility that I can effectively express the intellectual and personal gratitude I owe, I should like here to acknowledge my teachers, colleagues, and friends: Nguyen Bac, Ngo Nhu Binh, Nguyen Nguyet Cam, Kathy Charlton, Pham Van Chuong, Dan Duffy, Mary and Michael Etherton, Peter Geithner, Murray Hiebert, Nguyen Thai Yen Huong, Neil Jamieson, Minh and Fred Kauffman, Tim Karr, Viet Huong and Jim Kurtz, Vu Ky, the late Le Mai (a man of true greatness), John McAuliff and Mary McDonnell, David Marr, Do Xuan Oanh, Nguyen Xuan Phong, Bui Thanh Son, Dao Spencer, Le Thi, Le Thi Nham Tuyet, Phan Nguyen Toan, Steve Wheatley,

Peter Zinoman, and Mary Zurbuchen. For detailed discussions on Hanoi, I am grateful to Kathy Charlton, Christina Dodd, Tim Karr, Annalise Koeman, and Phan Nguyen Toan. I also wish to thank Curtis Brown, Ltd. for permission to quote from Harrison Salisbury's *Behind the Lines* (copyright 1967).

This volume is dedicated with love to Margaret, Rosy, and Thea.

MARK SIDEL

Iowa
February 1998

Contents

1
The Early History of Hanoi

The site is large and flat, the fields high and well enough exposed. The population is protected against high water and floods. Everything there flourishes and prospers. It is a most beautiful site where men and riches from the four cardinal points converge, and it is an excellent capital for [a] royal dynasty of ten thousand generations. I wish there for [to] take advantage of this favourable terrain and establish the capital there. What do you think, mandarins of the Court?

(Anon., 1010, reprinted 1977b)

THE graceful national capital of Hanoi had inauspicious beginnings. At the same site where present-day Hanoi stands, between what is the West Lake and the Red River, stood a small agricultural and fishing village by about 2000 BC. Archaeological investigations by Vietnamese scholars reveal a fairly diversified culture, encompassing agricultural cultivation, livestock breeding, fishing, hunting, handicraft and pottery production, copper and iron smelting, and bronze engraving. Archaeology has revealed the daily life of the earliest residents of Hanoi: '[B]ronze plough shares, spades, scythes; custard apple and caranium seeds, burnt paddy seeds and rice husk; stone and bronze axes, bronze knives and arrows; and stone and terracotta weights for fishing nets' (Nguyen Vinh Phuc, 1995). Vietnamese historians even paint a picture of how early inhabitants may have appeared.

From the figures engraved on the drums and other objects made of bronze, one can get an idea of life in that period: people lived in houses built on stilts the roofs of which were turned up like swallow-tailed pirogues, and in which the staircase was in the middle. Boat transport on rivers and lake was widespread. So far as dress is concerned, bronze objects unearthed at Trung Mau show human figures wearing a kind of poncho and head-dress adorned with feathers (Tran Quoc Vuong and Nguyen Vinh Long, 1977a).

1

Ethnic tribes occupied the area known as Hanoi as early as 2000 BC. In this region a local military leader named Thuc Phan established a regional capital in the third century BC, and the defence installation he built at Co Loa, located in what is now the suburbs of Hanoi, is among the earliest physical site still visible in the city. The Co Loa Citadel was a series of defence walls surrounded by a moat (Colour Plate 1). Some of those ramparts remain, along with temples commemorating the first ruler to have made Hanoi a capital. Thuc Phan, also known as An Duong Vuong, defended the village capital against attack by the Chinese emperor's forces in 218 BC, the first of many times Hanoi would be defended against invaders, and the beginnings of its proud history as a centre of resistance.

After the Han Chinese invaded and gained control in 208–207 BC the village we now call the city of Hanoi came under Chinese control and remained under varying degrees of Chinese suzerainty for over a thousand years. In the early seventh century the Hanoi area became the administrative seat for northern Vietnam. New fortifications were constructed in the seventh and eighth centuries, and an intricate citadel named Dai La was completed in the ninth century. By the tenth century, according to Vietnamese historians, the site then called Tong Binh 'had 50,000 inhabitants, not including the garrisoned Chinese troops and the Chinese administrators. The citadel was typical of the period: not so much a town as a fortress' (Tran Quoc Vuong and Nguyen Vinh Long, 1977a).

When Chinese rule was weakened in the tenth century, following numerous rebellions, the early Vietnamese kings shifted the capital to a more easily defended site outside the present Hanoi. But in 1010 King Ly Thai To revisited the Dai La Citadel and, unhappy with the current capital, the home of fallen dynasties, transferred his capital back to Dai La, which is now Hanoi. The new capital was given the name Thang Long (Soaring Dragon), from a legend that spoke of a golden dragon rising from the Dai La Citadel. The 'Royal Edict on the Transfer of the Capital' issued by Ly Thai To in 1010 survives, and its resonance of pride in place echoes down to our times.

The two dynasties of the Dinh [968–980] and the Le [980–1009] ... followed ... only the dictates of pleasure, ignoring the will of Heaven. They stubbornly remained in this place. Their dynasties were short-lived, their fate tenuous. The one hundred families [the people] were ruined while the millions of resources remained scarcely utilized. This causes the great suffering and I feel obliged to transfer the capital. Even more so because Dai La [the current day Hanoi], the ancient capital of His Highness Cao [proconsul of the Tang Dynasty and builder of Dai La], is situated in the heart of our country. It has topographical features resembling a coiled dragon or a crouching tiger. The capital is laid out on a North-South East-West axis, and is favorably situated with regard to the mountains and rivers.

The site is large and flat, the fields high and well enough exposed. The population is protected against high water and floods. Everything there flourishes and prospers. It is a most beautiful site where men and riches from the four cardinal points converge, and it is an excellent capital for [a] royal dynasty of ten thousand generations. I wish there for take advantage of this favourable terrain and establish the capital there. What do you think, mandarins of the Court? (Anon., 1010, reprinted 1977b).

The designation of Thang Long as Ly Thai To's capital had significant effects on Thang Long's growth throughout the Ly Dynasty (1009–1225). Dikes and cosmological mounds were built befitting a capital. The chronicler Le Huu Trac wrote of the dikes in the eighteenth century that 'horse carts could move along them easily'; that was true even earlier, and remains the case to the present. Some of these are still visible. Dikes have been built or reinforced almost continuously since the eleventh century.

The dikes then and now remain crucial protectors of the city's physical integrity, and the control of water is a dominant theme in the history of Hanoi. To this day residents who endanger the dikes, as a number of landowners did in the early 1990s by constructing large residences on the dikes themselves, are subject to severe punishment by the authorities. An old poem extolled the waters of Hanoi and of the To River, which meets the Red River to create the 'city between the rivers' or Hanoi (Plate 1).

1. Paul Doumer Bridge over the Red River, early 1900s.
    (Nguyen Hong Sam)

The To River water is pure and cool.
I bring my sampan close to yours,
Trying to show my feeling with my oars
Like the To Lich water my love flows deep.

(Tran Quoc Vuong and Nguyen Vinh Long, 1977a)

In addition to dikes and mounds, the city was redesigned in
1010. The inner part of the city was designated the Royal City or
'Hoang Thanh' and the concentric area around it the Commoners'
City or 'Kinh Thanh'. Within the Royal City stood the Royal

4

Palace or 'Cam Thanh', where the king, queens, and concubines resided. Both the Royal City and the Royal Palace were protected by intricate systems of gates, walls, and moats. Outside each of the four main gates stood the large markets and residential areas of the capital, divided geographically by guilds. Several of the temples and other structures built within this commoners' area survive to the present day.

The Royal City was constructed in the eleventh and twelfth centuries and included a sizeable four storey palace and other residences, meeting halls, pagodas, royal gardens, and small lakes. Many of the buildings were built in the centuries after 1010. The Royal Palace, of which no structures survive to the present day, is known to us only through the work of historians, archaeologists, and poets. 'Access was forbidden to everybody, even to the highest courtiers and the crown prince, without a specific order from the [Emperor].' The emperor, his queens, and concubines spent their days and nights in a spacious palace of four storeys 'made of vermillion lacquered wood, with columns adorned with gold painted dragons, dancing fairies and engraved ibises', as well as in the other smaller palace residences. The Can Nguyen Palace, also within the Royal Palace compound, was used for audiences and discussions with government officials. Although the Royal Palace no longer exists, throughout the first half of the twentieth century ordinary residents of Hanoi continued to unearth bricks, foundation stones with carvings of dragons and phoenixes, pottery, porcelain, and other relics of imperial life in a forbidden city (Tran Quoc Vuong and Nguyen Vinh Long, 1997a).

The Commoners' City was the residential and commercial centre for ordinary people, soldiers, and government officials. Pagodas, some heavily rebuilt, survive from this era. A series of pagodas, temples, and monuments were built around the city during and after the eleventh century, and many survive. They include, perhaps most prominently, Van Mieu (Temple of Literature) in western central Hanoi, a Confucian temple still standing on well-kept grounds (Colour Plate 2). The Quoc Tu Giam (National Academy), the government school and examination ground for Confucian scholars, originally built as a prince's study hall, was located within the Temple of Literature.

2. Hanoi street scene, early twentieth century. (Nguyen Hong Sam)

Several of Hanoi's present-day large covered markets stand at traditional sites outside the four main gates to the former Royal City. The Cua Nam market, for example, which still operates daily, is situated directly outside what was the South Gate. And a series of Buddhist temples, also built during the Ly era, reflect Buddhism's important religious and cultural role for ordinary citizens and royalty alike. Many of those temples and pagodas, including the Tran Quoc Temple and the Chua Mot Cot (One Pillar Pagoda), still stand, though they have been significantly reconstructed. Several are still used for Buddhist ceremonies.

Administration of the city during the Ly and later dynasties was carried out by a royally appointed governor and hundreds of officials. The importance of governing Thang Long, already clear in the Ly Dynasty, has carried down directly through the French colonial era and into Hanoi in the post-1954 era of independence. So, too, has the monarchic, and later colonial, emphasis on the preservation of security in the capital. Royal and municipal guard companies were founded in the Ly and Tran dynasties, and through the French colonial era to this day the security of the capital and within the city remains an important facet of social and political life in Hanoi.

The physical and administrative development of Hanoi beginning with the Ly Dynasty in 1010 remain relatively clear, even many centuries later. But we know fairly little of daily life in Hanoi during this period. Royal life took place within the Royal City and the Royal Palace, and the life of commerce, scholarship, and military affairs took place largely in the Commoners' City outside. The patterns of social life in this then small but important city are harder to understand clearly. Vietnamese historians have struggled with the social history of their capital.

To describe life in old Thang Long is no easy task. Vietnamese books of the time recorded only political events and change at the royal courts, and neglected social and economic accounts and events. With the early appearance of a centralized feudal state, the scholars in those days often had only a general view of the situation in the country, and paid little attention to local conditions and places including Thang Long (Tao Trang and The Hung, 1977).

At its ascendancy Hanoi was divided administratively into *phuong* (guilds) and *pho* (streets) (Plate 2). The *phuong* was the key administrative unit in urban life, similar to an urban district or rural commune today. Police and the administrative apparatus operated at the *phuong* level and below, directed from above. Trades were concentrated at the *pho* level, and the most concentrated area was in the thirty-six guild streets (the old quarter) at the northern end of the city. While the specialty trades once practised along the streets for which such trades are named have now dispersed, the street names remain evocative symbols of life in old Hanoi, and the ancient quarter is amongst the proudest symbols of a proud city. As an old Hanoi folk verse goes:

The thirty six streets of Hanoi
Hang Gao, Hang Duong, Hang Muoi, all pure
Each day we hold them in our hearts
Once acquainted they cannot be forgotten
When we make a friend or lose a friend we all come here.

(Giang Quan, 1994)

It has been argued that the *phuong* structure, in which residents came originally from a common village or other defined area, and the trading emphasis of the Commoners' City as differentiated from the administrative and military aspects of the Royal City, helped to promote cohesion in the Hanoi of this period. Today that may be difficult to judge, but the physical and architectural legacy of the *phuong* and of the trading city remain visible, represented in their clearest form in Hanoi's old quarter.

Hanoi has long seemed a proud city to the foreign visitor, and these dynastic periods in which it was capital were among its prouder moments. An anonymous Vietnamese poet put it this way:

Fragrant are the soi and the jasmine flowers,
Clever are the people in the capital city,
Can you say that jasmine flowers are not fragrant,
That capital city people are not refined?

(Tran Quoc Vuong and Nguyen Vinh Long, 1977b)

Beginning in 1010 and until the fifteenth century, through three dynasties, numerous uprisings, and Mongol invasions and incursions, Thang Long remained the capital and administrative seat of northern Vietnam. Much of the pagoda and temple construction which defines and graces Hanoi today has its roots in the Ly Dynasty of the eleventh century. During the Tran Dynasty (1226–1400), foreign and non-Chinese traders began to arrive in Thang Long, and some foreigners took up residence in the city. They included Uighurs, Indians, and Javanese, in addition to the Chinese. And during the latter half of the thirteenth century, Ming Dynasty invading forces occupied the capital.

In 1407 the Chinese returned but maintained Thang Long as their capital under the name Dong Quan. And when Le Loi and his Vietnamese troops defeated the Ming Dynasty's occupying forces in 1428, the new Le Dynasty again maintained Thang Long as the capital.

The Le Dynasty (1428–1768) restored the Royal City and expanded it so that by 1490 it covered the area of the former Royal and Commoners' cities. Although construction tapered off in the late sixteenth century, a century later foreign visitors marvelled at the expanded Royal City.

The ruins of the triple wall of the old city and the old palace give a good idea of what they contained in the height of their splendour. The Palace alone enclosed an area of six to seven miles in circumference. Its yards were paved with marble, its gates and the remains of its apartments testify to its former magnificence (Baron, 1685).

The Jesuit priest J. P. de Marini also visited Thang Long, which the Le Dynasty called Dong Kinh in the late seventeenth century, and his impressions of the city survive.

The number of sentries, officers, workmen and people of all nationalities who work there; the order, the clothes, the gardens, elephants, horses, the weapons and other munitions are astonishing, beyond imagination. Although the King's apartments are built of wood, the gold and embroidered ornaments, the fine mats of different colours as well as the rich carpets, render them incomparable. In the palace in which the Bua (King) lives there are also large stone arcades and extraordinarily thick walls. It is built on a forest of solid stilts, and a flight of steps leads to its one storey.... The rooms are spacious, the galleries are covered and the large court yards stretch out endlessly (J. P. de Marini, 1666; translated in Vuong and Long, 1977).

And Vietnamese visitors marvelled at the West Lake.

The boat emerges from below a small mountain and enters the lake. There before your eyes is a vast expanse of blue sky and rippling green water. Groups of white storks wheel over the lake, teals scud the waves in couples near the opposite bank; on the side of the dyke, the thick foliage of the Ly Cung palace sways in the wind, back and forth, flattening and straightening. On the small islands in the middle of the lake is a row of palaces (Tran Quoc Vuong and Nguyen Vinh Vong, 1977a).

Foreign traders and residents increased in the seventeenth and eighteen centuries, and it was their pronunciation of Dong Kinh that created the term Tonkin (Tonking or Tonquin) by which the French and others would refer to northern Vietnam for the next several hundred years. But as the old waned the new was emerging. While palaces lay in ruins, Hanoi in the seventeenth and eighteenth centuries was becoming a more modern commercial centre.

Another western visitor provided a description of the sense of activity in the city.

The city is 6,000 feet long and 6,000 feet wide, and its streets are so wide that from ten to twelve horsemen can easily ride along them abreast. But twice a month, at the new moon and full moon, there are so many people coming and going, crowding all the streets, that one is continuously jostled and pushed, and it takes much time to get very little way (Rhodes, 1651).

The British sailor William Dampier, who visited Hanoi (also then known as Cachao) in 1688, recorded his impressions as well.

The Capital City Cachao, which stands in the high Country about 80 Miles from the Sea, on the West-side of the River, and on a pretty level, yet rising Ground, lies open … without wall, bank or ditch. There may be in Cachao about 20,000 Houses. The Houses are generally low, the walls of the Houses are of mud, and the covering Thatch, yet some are built with Brick, and the covering with Pan-tile.

The principal Streets in this City are very wide, though some are but narrow. They are most of them pav'd, or patch'd rather, with small Stones; but after a very ill manner. In the wet Season they are very dirty; and in the dry Time there are many fragrant Ponds.

The Kings of Tonquin, who make this City their constant Resident, have two or three Palaces in it, such as they be. Two of them are very mean; they are built with Timber, yet have they many great Guns planted in Houses near them, Stables for the King's Elephants and Horses, and pretty large square Spots of Ground for the soldiers to draw themselves up regularly before him. The Third Palace is called the Palace Royal. It is more magnificently built than the other two.... The Wall that incompasseth it is most remarkable.

Many traders and handicrafts specialists moved into Hanoi from nearby areas, helping to create a commodity economy in the Hanoi area, perhaps for the first time in its history. This rapid increase in trade and economic activity diluted the concentration of guild and trade activities along specific *pho*. One street might originally have been the centre for lacquer work, or bookbinding, but economic activity in the seventeenth and eighteenth centuries spread many trades around the city. A visual image of the non-royal sections of Hanoi before the arrival of the French may not be easy to conjure up, but the French architectural historian Christian Pedelahore (1986) has provided one evocation.

Most accounts by foreign travelers, explorers, missionaries and a few engravings present old Hanoi as a low town with houses built mainly of light materials (walls of woven bamboo, thatch roofs): sites of handicraft production and places for selling, stocking and habitation lining narrow winding lanes.... [T]he trading quarters ... were situated ... between the citadel and the river. Unlike the citadel with sparse constructions and trees in abundance, the trading town, as shown in a number of engravings, had large built-up areas, with the presence of vegetal building materials. Water was found everywhere, even apparently forming a central kernel (pools and ponds) around which 'islets' would come into existence along the lanes.

Construction first tapered off and much was destroyed in the strife of the seventeenth and eighteenth centuries, especially in 1786, when the Le emperor ordered the palaces of the Trinh lords in Thang Long destroyed. After a long period of rebellion and internal strife, the southern-led Nguyen Dynasty came to power in 1802 and moved the capital south to Hue. Since the term 'Long' in the name Thang Long (City of the Soaring Dragon) was considered a royal symbol, the first Nguyen emperor, Gia Long, changed the city's name to Thang Thinh, and then to Hanoi (meaning the city between the rivers). Emperor Gia Long was familiar with the work of the French military engineer Vauban, a then well-known architect of citadels and fortresses. Emperor Gia Long downgraded Hanoi to a local capital and reduced its size to a smaller citadel, with five gates but none facing south, 'perhaps to prevent all malevolent gazing towards the royal court of Hue' (Tran Quoc Vuong and Nguyen Vinh Vong, 1977a).

Much of the glory of Hanoi seemed past. A poet's lament captured the scene:

The soul of autumn grass hovers over the tracks of carriages and horses of bygone days,
A waning light from the setting sun catches the foundations of former palaces.

(Tao Trang and The Hung, 1977)

As the nineteenth century began, royal life was centred in Hue, but Hanoi's social and economic life continued to thrive. The guilds and trades expanded, markets became more and more active and came to constitute 'an essential element in Thang Long's economic structure', as Vietnamese historian Nguyen Thua Hy (1985) has put it. Streets were paved and widened. Houses of sturdier construction were built in the old Commoners' City. And the Red River and its tributaries continued to play a crucial role in the development of Hanoi's commerce and handicrafts distribution. Despite the reduction of its political role, Hanoi remained a commercial and social hub (Plate 3). Its political and diplomatic role never truly ceased even though the Nguyen Dynasty formally moved the capital to Hue.

Most trade was to and from areas near Hanoi. A certain amount of 'foreign trade' was conducted with visiting French, Dutch, British, Spanish, and other merchants, but on a reasonably small scale, mostly secret to evade imperial prohibitions on private foreign trade.

3. A Hanoi religious gathering, late nineteenth century. (Nguyen Hong Sam)

From 1802 to 1882 Hanoi continued to develop. Small-scale commerce and handicrafts led to economic development as the city swelled to perhaps 100,000–150,000 by the second half of the nineteenth century. In 1812, the Nguyen Dynasty built the Flag Tower just outside the Citadel which still stands today. The tower is currently within the grounds of the Army Museum (Colour Plate 3) in central Hanoi and may be climbed by visitors. Its foundations and brickwork have been repaired but the structure remains as constructed in 1812.

A later Nguyen Dynasty emperor, Minh Mang, forced to come north from Hue to Thang Long in 1820 to meet a Chinese envoy who recognized no other capital, merged the city and its outlying districts in 1831 and termed the resulting province-level unit Hanoi, the 'city within the rivers'. According to Tran Quoc Vuong, Nguyen Vinh Phuc, and other Vietnamese historians, this event marks an early use of the term Hanoi for the city. The Emperor Minh Mang, according to Vietnamese historians, 'either removed to Hue or destroyed on the spot all royal buildings: the Royal Palace, the temple to Royal Ancestors, the temple of Heaven, the mound for worship of Heaven and Earth, and many more' (Anon., 1977a). The next Nguyen emperor, Tu Duc, further reduced the importance of the old Royal City by demolishing the royal palaces and removing many articles to Hue for installation in the royal capital there. The reduction in Hanoi's role was evoked and lamented by the nineteenth-century poet Nguyen Cong Tru (1977):

Whether it is blossom time or not, jasmine is always jasmine
Elegant or not, one is nevertheless a citizen of the capital.
We look back, and think, alas, was [it] there that songs and dances
    resounded,
When this land was capital of the empire
When these hills, these waters were its sublime environment
For the dynasties to build up their empires under Viet Nam's skies.
In the hamlets here, folk display urban elegance.
The metropolis still has forests
And over the rolling plain resounds the buffalo herd's song.
In the water wafting fishermen's sails are mirrored.

The grass and flowers open and wither,
The hills and rivers smile at growth and decline,
Nature has witnessed many upheavals.
The pensive traveller wonders how many times
The stars in the sky have changed,
Where now are the royal palaces and imperial temples of yore?
The gibbon exults, the oriole warbles not without irony.

Despite the de-emphasis the Nguyen Dynasty placed on Hanoi, other landmarks were built or restored, sometimes with private funds. For example, the small pagoda which graces the even smaller island in the Ho Hoan Kiem (Lake of the Restored Sword) in downtown Hanoi was built in 1865. Known as the Ngoc Son Temple and currently a significant site along the Ho Hoan Kiem, the 1865 construction included the small bridge which connects the lake side with the temple. And, as Tran Quoc Vuong and Nguyen Vinh Phuc have observed, 'Pen Tower and Inkslab Mound were erected in front of the temple gate, testifying to the respect of the population of the old capital for education' (Tran Quoc Vuong and Nguyen Vinh Vong, 1977). By 1882 Hanoi would be a worthy prize for the French as the Vietnamese colonial era dawned (Plate 4).

4. Hanoi street trade, early twentieth century. (Nguyen Hong Sam)

2
Hanoi under French Colonization, 1882–1945

FRANCE colonized most of southern Vietnam in 1864, and French military forces moved to occupy Hanoi in 1873, but it was not until 1884 that Hanoi was fully occupied by the French. A French protectorate was established for northern Vietnam (Tonkin) in 1884, with its headquarters at Hanoi. The colonization was prolonged and violent, and followed many years of trade, missionary activity, and military expeditions. As British competitors in trade and colonization put it, '[L]ike ourselves ... the French have gone forward with the Bible in one hand and the Gatling gun in the other, and if the natives did not accept one he got the other' (*Straits Budget*, 1907).

French control of Hanoi would remain a significant theme for the next seventy years, and strong popular and intellectual opposition to French colonial rule would frequently surface, with Hanoi as a centre of that opposition. But Hanoi was also the centre for French administrative control for Vietnam and all of Indo-China (as it was then termed), and French colonization had deep and powerful effects on the political, social, economic as well as architectural and other spheres of life in Hanoi.

The French colonization of Indo-China, and of Hanoi, resulted in massive social and economic changes as well. French officials dominated administrative agencies and political decision-making. A small intellectual class began to appear in the late nineteenth century, and intellectual and armed rebellion was frequent until the French gave up rule in 1954 (Marr, 1971 and 1981). Indigenous clerks and officials joined the overstaffed and incompetent French colonial civil service. And under French colonial capitalism the number of urban workers, craftsmen, and traders increased rapidly as well, fuelled by significant migration of poor peasants into the colonial centres, the cities. The scholars and translators Greg and Monique Lockhart have noted that Hanoi had a very large floating population, about 75,000 in 1921 and about 180,000 in 1937, a significant portion of the population. These economic and social processes inspired a new kind of literature in Hanoi, urban reportage, that chronicled in evocative and often dramatic fashion the tribulations of Hanoi's new working class of rickshaw pullers, household servants, and other poorly paid workers (Lockhart and Lockhart, 1996).

Colonialism and increasing class differentiation was clearly reflected in changed social relationships as well (Plate 5). Tam Lang, a journalist who chronicled life as a rickshaw puller, learned that clearly.

If you pull an old person, you have to call on people to keep out of the way as you run slowly; pulling a Frenchman, you have to run strongly and not be afraid even at night when the street lamps are slow to come on; pulling rich young ladies and gentlemen, you must run with a sense of

5. French automobiles and Vietnamese rickshaws, early twentieth century. (Nguyen Hong Sam)

16

importance. In other words, it depends on the kind of passenger you have.... [I]f you have one that looks down on you as an inferior, you have to keep your mouth shut; a passenger who is not a mandarin still has be be treated like one (Lockhart and Lockhart, 1996).

Social and Architectural Transformation under the French

Hanoi as the French found it in 1873 was, as Andre Masson (1929) put it,

a composite agglomeration where an administrative capital, a commercial town and numerous villages were juxtaposed within the same enclosure. The Citadel, two or three times more extensive than what we designate with this word today, constituted the administrative capital where the provincial mandarins, the representatives of the Emperor, resided. The commercial town, densely populated and confined between the Red River and the Citadel, was itself divided into a Chinese quarter of affluent merchants and an Annamese quarter of small artisans.

The initial period of French control of a part of Hanoi (1875–82) resulted in their control of a small concession area near the bank of the Red River, south and east of the current centre of Hanoi. After the battles of 1882, the French gained control of the Citadel in the centre of the city. And the French remaking of Hanoi began, perhaps not surprisingly, with what Christian Pedelahore (1986) has termed 'the symbolic and real destruction of royal power and its physical materialization: the fortified citadel; and its replacement, equally symbolic, by military barracks and depots'. The Citadel was virtually destroyed in the years following the establishment of the French protectorate, but the trading, or commercial areas of Hanoi were not destroyed. And in place of the Citadel a colonial capital was envisioned that would express the power and (for the French) the superiority of France.

France made its influence felt almost immediately in Hanoi's architecture and townscape as well as in its political and administrative life, especially after France's first civilian governor, Paul Bert, arrived in 1886. For, as Pedelahore (1986) has written of French attitudes toward Hanoi and other Vietnamese cities,

[t]he main places for the diffusion of European economic and cultural models were to be the cities, which would become 'command posts' of all colonial activities.... Indeed, if colonial space came to be regarded as a direct extension of the metropolitan country and no longer as an 'exotic far-away place', it was essentially for ideological and economic reasons (massive diffusion of a close-circuit market) and for propaganda (massive diffusion of the image of 'Great France'). And if the land was subjected to experimentation, it was because, fundamentally, colonial space was regarded as virgin land with no hindrance—pre-colonial rights being essentially ignored—where the population could be shaped and regrouped at will.

How was this ideology expressed in the remaking of Hanoi? In addition to the construction of broad boulevards and strong physical changes to the map of the city, two types of structures dominated construction in the early decades of French colonization of Hanoi. The first, and less important, was functionalist models of French military construction that began to be built in 1873, when more permanent military bases were established in Hanoi. Perhaps ironically, local climatic and topographical conditions had to be taken into account in the construction of some of these military barracks and depots, perhaps presaging one future strand in the development of French architecture and construction in northern Vietnam.

The second, and more important, was neo-classical, Parisian administration buildings erected by the colonial administrators as symbols of French authority and power, particularly in the last years of the nineteenth century and the first years of the twentieth (Colour Plate 4). These were 'invested with an important symbolic function ... [for] "the authority of the French Resident must be seen and felt...." [A]rchitecture was ... assigned an important role, ... a role of representation and materialization of colonial power and superiority' (Pedelahore, 1986). Thus in the first phase of French construction, from 1884 through the early twentieth century, four broad avenues were laid out—Paul Bert (Trang Tien), Rollandes (Hai Ba Trung), Carreau (Ly Thuong Kiet), and Gambetta (Tran Hung Dao). At the turn of the century a number of important buildings were constructed in French neo-classical style. These included the Palace of the Governor-General, the Opera House (Colour Plate 5), the Palace and Office of the French Resident, the St Joseph's Cathedral, the Metropole Hotel, the Hanoi Railway Station (Plate 6), the Railway Administration head-quarters, the main post office, the Doumer (Long Bien) Bridge, and the Dong Xuan Market (Plate 7). Many of these were designed closely after similar buildings in Paris (Wright, 1991).

These were constructions of power, but one of the most ostenta-tious of these no longer exists. Early in this century Governor Paul Doumer commissioned a Grand Exposition Hall of Hanoi that was completed in time to house the Hanoi Exposition of 1902. This extraordinary neo-classical building, over 100 metres long and columned, survives only in pictures, but at that time its construc-tion was a great event. Christian Pedelahore (1986) has written that its huge cost caused a deficit in the colonial budget for Hanoi for more than ten years, all in the pursuit of a 'policy of prestige, which was aimed at making the capital of Indochina a small Paris, seriously weigh[ing] on the pursuit of continuous development'.

During the Second World War the Grand Exposition Hall of

6. Early view of the Hanoi Railway Station. (Nguyen Hong Sam)

19

7. Dong Xuan Market in the 1930s. (Nguyen Hong Sam)

Hanoi was used by the Japanese as a billet for soldiers and then bombed by the American forces. After a number of years as an open air theatre, the Soviet–Vietnamese Friendship Cultural Palace (Colour Plate 6), an uninspiring large edifice, was built on the site in the early 1980s.

Numerous villas were also constructed for French residents of Hanoi during this period (Plate 8). And these, too, were based on a familiar pattern.

The main building faced the entrance gate of the plot.... Behind it, generally abutting on the enclosure, were the service places: kitchen, laundry, storehouse.... This secondary part of the habitation was the place where indigenous servants worked and lived. Thus, in its spatial lay-out each unit of the colonial quarter repeated within its walls the spatial separation which characterized the city. In the foreground, the wide, light, functional and hygienic living space of the French colonist. In the background, the narrow space, the dark and dirty places for the native (Pedelahore, 1986).

These architectural patterns, it may be noted, would eventually serve Vietnamese rebels as well. Nguyen Bac, a Communist cadre who infiltrated Hanoi in the early 1950s to work among intellectual and cultural figures during the French occupation, tells of

8. French villa, later government offices, c.1920. (Nguyen Hong Sam)

living with sympathetic Vietnamese servants in the basement service areas of French villas. The separate lives of foreground and background, of upstairs and downstairs, took on a humour in his tales of outfoxing the French colonists, both villa owners and security police. It was a humour moderated only by the knowledge of the torture, imprisonment, and possible death that awaited a Communist agent and his servant protector if caught by the French security police while hiding out in the home of a French businessman or government official.

I was relatively safe [in] the house of Mr. Hop, a servant on Carnot Street (Phan Dinh Phung). This was the house of a big landowner who was also a horse breeder, named De Monpezat. He lived upstairs and his servant lived in the basement.... The owner never came down to the servant's quarters.... When the owner left the house I went upstairs to listen to the radio. When the car returned a bell would sound, the servant would open the gate, and I would have enough time to go downstairs.

Once steel-helmeted police encircled the house in the middle of the night, while De Monpezat was smoking opium upstairs. Hearing the sound of the whistles, he hurried out onto the balcony, upbraiding

21

the police with 'Dirty dog, dirty dog'. The squad of police had to withdraw at once, as I lay peacefully in the house. This was a very safe place, and I could live there happily.

I gave money to Mr. Hop for food, but he said merrily: 'The Frenchman is feeding you, I'm not feeding you!' Here there was coffee every morning and I could eat beefsteak with fried potatoes. This was the time I ate the best (Nguyen Bac, 1994).

One senior French architect, Paulin Vial, saw his project as 'a tremendous work[,] the renovation of an ancient city which was to be recomposed, made wholesome, exposed to air and light, without destroying the most interesting wrecks [*sic*] of its past' (Masson, 1929). A more cynical vision of Hanoi was found, perhaps not surprisingly, by a British visitor writing in the early twentieth century:

Hanoi is an administrative town and little else. It is stuffed with a host of fonctionnaires, big and little, who lick stamps by day and then go home and tick off the hours to their pensions.... The villas are pure French, making no concessions to climate, and were it not for palms, bougainvillea, etc., they might be standing in some pleasant outskirt of Paris—Neuilly, for instance (Garstin, 1928).

The neo-classical style was the rule in government buildings and villas until the 1920s, when the pattern of design began to change and a new, or 'oriental' or 'Indo-chinese' style came into vogue. The famous French architect Ernest Hebrard, who arrived in Hanoi in 1923, embodied and promoted this shift, one in which

constructions underwent an evolution towards spatial forms better adapted to the climatic conditions (sunshine, monsoon …) of the country, and in agreement with new hygienic and rationalist ideas: adoption of the veranda, roofs jutting out, double windows (view and light provided by the lower part, ventilation by the upper part).... Hebrard was illustrative of the 'limited opening' which characterized part of the colonial power in the thirties (Pedelahore, 1986).

Hebrard sought to link indigenous design elements with representations of colonial power. As Gwendolyn Wright explained, government buildings and some private villas began to employ 'oriental' or traditional Vietnamese style elements as well as French elements under the new 'policy of association … requiring a visible attention to the needs and traditions of the colonized peoples'. 'Public architecture', as Wright (1991) explains the French view of the time, 'implied that French functionaries appreciated traditional Indochinese cultures, that colonialism would preserve and even advance these other cultures in an equitable manner.'

Three significant buildings, each still standing in Hanoi, exemplify this shift in design focus. The Louis Finot Museum and L'École Française d'Extrême Orient, the primary French research centre specializing in Indo-China, built on what is now Pham Ngu Lao Street, was completed in 1925. It now serves as the National History Museum (Colour Plate 7). The main building of Hanoi University was built nearby, completed in 1926 (Plate 9). The French Financial Service headquarters, completed in 1931 on what is now Ba Dinh Square and which now houses the Vietnamese Ministry of Foreign Affairs, is perhaps the most striking example of the use of Indo-Chinese design elements. Hebrard sought 'a scholarly

9. Main building of Hanoi University, with rickshaws in front, c.1915. (Nguyen Hong Sam)

hybrid architecture, both localist and international', aiming to 'rewin the hearts and ... integrate ... the Vietnamese intellectual elites and the bourgeoisie' (Pedelahore, 1986). His new buildings exhibited more careful planning of the relationship between the structures and their neighbours, on a smaller scale, with better ventilation (which Hebrard and his colleagues learned from local practices) (Wright, 1991).

Hebrard also elaborated general plans for Hanoi, Saigon, Phnom Penh, and Dalat, part of an attempt to unify and compose the cities of the colonial empire. While Hebrard continues to be regarded in Hanoi as an architect and planner of colonialism, he is also recognized as the first person to formulate a general plan for the layout and development of Hanoi, one that through colonial power and construction lives on to this day, even though substantial portions of Hebrard's vision were not realized because of financial difficulties in Paris and in the Indo-Chinese colony.

Increased export earnings was the main economic goal of French colonization in Indo-China, and opium revenues served as the primary source of funding for the Indo-Chinese colonial budget. But budgetary resources even to support the representation of French power and the promotion of export were not infinite, while the buildings Hebrard and his predecessors and successors had proposed were very expensive. Political events also curtailed planning and building (Wright, 1991; Descours-Gatin, 1992).

Hebrard's plans and his elaboration of a mixed 'Indo-Chinese' style influenced several generations of Vietnamese and French architects and planners. And with the founding of the architecture section of l'Ecole des Beaux Arts de l'Indochina in 1927, several generations of French-influenced Vietnamese architects were trained between the late 1920s and 1945.

For Hebrard and his French colleagues, the remaking of Hanoi was a project with multiple goals. One was clearly to project and maintain French power over an intractable colony split into different cultural, ethnic, and linguistic groups, increasingly opposed by indigenous intellectuals and others. And as Gwendolyn Wright and Christian Pedelahore have claimed, Hebrard and his contemporaries' turn toward including indigenous Vietnamese elements in architecture and design in the 1920s and 1930s was an attempt to mollify, attract, and seek the support of sectors of the Vietnamese intelligentsia and the new, if small, bourgeoisie. But Hebrard was also engaged in a broader dialogue with French-based urban planners and architects over the shape of modern cities and their structures, a debate that while beyond the scope of this short work is of importance and is worthy of mention. 'If Hebrard's buildings used local motifs, these resulted primarily from climatic and other functional considerations.... Hebrard wanted to use history and a certain cultural sensibility in order to infuse fresh vitality into French architecture.... In his view of culture, French aesthetic leadership and tutelage paralleled the political superiority of the colonial government over its "native charges"' (Wright, 1991). As Hebrard said at a Paris conference, '[I]nstead of building in Indochina pastiches of what exists in Europe, why not direct the natives along a path that accords well with their traditions, their temperaments, and their aptitudes, making them evolve normally toward a modern art that will be particular to them?' (Wright, 1991).

For all the planning and construction of Hanoi (Plate 10)

10. Paul Doumer (Long Bien) Bridge, late nineteenth century. (Nguyen Hong Sam)

between the 1880s and the 1940s, there was also intense criticism of the French effort both in the colony and in France. In France, criticism focused on the earlier neo-classical, particularly grandiose, efforts. Wright quotes a member of the French Academy who criticized the Hanoi Opera House, an early neo-classical construction, as 'a pretentious caricature' of the Paris Opera. 'It is, moreover, a troubling symbol ... where all our faults come together: love of pleasure, of artifice, of the artificial, unreflective enthusiasm, and a careless lack of foresight' (Wright, 1991, quoting Eugene Brieux, 1910).

In Vietnam, there was deep resentment at the spending on great colonial buildings, regardless of form or style, and the virtually complete aversion to satisfying the daily needs of the millions of Vietnamese whose labour—and whose migration into the cities— fuelled the French export economy (Plate 11). And there was deep resentment at other aspects of French colonization as well—the imposed foreign structures of colonial power, the imposition of French thought and culture, the social relations of master and serf, and other issues. In 1937 about 20,000 French ran the Indo-Chinese colonial apparatus, ruling over some 19 million Vietnamese (Marr, 1981, citing Robequain, 1944).

In economic terms, French Indo-China, including the northern area surrounding Hanoi, was converted into 'a classic colony, her every economic fiber attuned to the demands of financial and industrial interests in France'. That classic colonial economy required massive agricultural exports (in the Vietnamese case, rubber and rice as the main crops), extensive mining and mineral exports, and significant imports of finished goods from French producers, all serving the French market and making it difficult for the local industry to stand on its feet. Conditions in the agricultural export sector, particularly in the rubber plantations controlled by the French, were extremely harsh. A growing Vietnamese urban *petit bourgeois* sector of traders, merchants, professionals, and related personnel symbolized the transition brought by French rule, and this sector also became among the most critical of that rule, and among the most active in exploring alternatives in Vietnam and beyond (Marr, 1971 and 1981).

11. Workers at a Hanoi local market, *c.*1920. (Nguyen Hong Sam)

Economic dislocation forced people to move from the country-side to the city. Thousands were attracted to the city's bright lights, as Vu Trong Phung describes.

Perhaps on nights when there are no moon and stars, the peasants in Nam Dinh, Thai Binh, Hai Duong, Bac Ninh, Son Tay and Hoa Binh go out into their courtyards and see a shining halo each time they turn their heads and look far-off into a corner of the sky. There, hovering over a thousand years of culture and glowing with easy riches, what the peasants see is the halo over Hanoi, and they are still leaving their villages for it! (Lockhart and Lockhart, 1996).

Most were disappointed, and large numbers ended up in abject poverty far from home.

When they left the country, they did not realize that they would find themselves in such a plight.... Dear Readers, just imagine Hanoi: street after street. And think of a very clumsy peasant lost in its labyrinth. Each street has houses, sidewalks, and footpaths, which means they all look alike and the roads appear to be never-ending. A peasant goes on and on;

he feels exhausted and stops. He's hungry but he can't eat, because he has no money. He wants to rest but can't lie down, because he can't pay for shelter (Lockhart and Lockhart, 1996).

The peasants and the urban destitute felt that desolation and alienation that comes with poverty. From what they saw on the streets of Hanoi and through journalism and the new writing movements, intellectuals and the petty bourgeoisie came to know it as well. Hanoi was fertile ground for new explorations and radical alternatives.

Despite French military, political, and economic power, and despite the willingness of large numbers of Vietnamese officials to collaborate with the colonizers, opposition grew virtually from the moment French colonization was complete, in 1885, until the French defeat in 1945 and the Democratic Republic of Vietnam was established. Much of the power of that opposition came from what historian David Marr (1971) has termed the 'anticolonial scholar-gentry', and much of the work of that scholar-gentry, later an active group of intellectuals, was centred in the large cities of French Indo-China, including Hanoi.

Leaders such as Phan Boi Chau and Phan Chu Trinh opposed the economic and political policies of French colonization, but they also began wrestling with how Vietnam should join the modern world. Hanoi was a centre for those dialogues and debates throughout the first half of the twentieth century. Those activities included a powerful Vietnamese language movement, the famous Association for the Dissemination of Quoc Ngu [Vietnamese] Study, intensive publishing activities that attempted to skirt French restraints, the activities of dozens of debate, education, charitable, and social organizations, as well as intensive explorations and debates on the role of women in a modern Vietnam. Beginning in the 1920s Hanoi was also a centre for the new reform theatre, which 'played a major role in disseminating new ideas and language beyond the intelligentsia' (Marr, 1981). Traditional Vietnamese popular theatre, Chinese opera, stage drama, and foreign films also flourished during the 1920s and 1930s. The city was also a centre for French repression of growing Vietnamese resistance, and for such famous trials as that of Phan Boi Chau in 1925. Perhaps most importantly, Hanoi was a key centre for the dialogues that involved the new *petit bourgeoisie* and the new intellectuals, among them journalists, teachers, translators, and writers, who led the resistance against the French and the explorations of new paths of culture, politics, and social life throughout the first five decades of the century under colonial rule.

3
Hanoi in War and Peace, 1945–1997

HANOI was a proud capital city in 1945 for those who opposed French colonialism, the centre of resistance to French colonial rule. The key battles for independence took place at sites that still stand in the city, such as the French-built Opera House and the Governor-General's residence in downtown Hanoi, where the ornate green fence surrounding the residence is still pock-marked with bullets from Vietnamese attacks on the French in August 1945.

One of Vietnam's most famous musicians and poets, Van Cao (1995), describes the chaotic summer of 1945, when Vietnamese rebels wrested Hanoi from French control.

Never another such time
In a life
Though leaves change on the trees of life
One clear summer like a string of pearls
Melancholy months and years
Dreams of longing
Of faith
They will never change
Always with humanity
Hungering only for love
Between brothers
A small space returns. Time closes again
One such summer
Never another.

But smaller, more localized acts of resistance, less well known than the major pitched battles in the streets, took place throughout the late 1930s and early 1940s in Hanoi as well, as young intellectuals organized in opposition to the French. One young student described the scene in her élite, French-run school in Hanoi in the early 1940s:

My sisters and I all studied at the Dong Khanh School in Hanoi, a school where all the students were girls and the teachers were all female.... But the discipline and order of the girls at Dong Khanh had already begun to change after the German Nazis occupied France. Marshall Petain had risen to power in France through German fascism. In 1941 and 1942, every day before we went in for class, we had to assemble on the school-yard to take part in the raising of the flags of France and Vietnam ... and listen to the French headmistress instruct and scold us.

We deliberately sabotaged the raising of the flags by hoisting the French flag more slowly than the Vietnamese flag, or by tangling the two flags so that they could not be raised.... We made the old hag of a headmistress frenzied with anger. And when we sang 'Marechal, nous voila, Devant toi, le sauveur de la France' (Marshal, we are here, before you, the savior of France) we sang it raggedly and unevenly (Le Thi, 1995).

On 2 September 1945, independence was declared in Ba Dinh Square, which was then a smaller gathering site. The Square was later expanded along Soviet design rules, with the Ho Chi Minh Mausoleum at its western edge and the headquarters of the Vietnamese Communist Party at its northern side in the old Lycee Albert Serraut.

The city suffered during the battle between the French and Ho Chi Minh's forces for control of northern Vietnam in late 1946 and early 1947.

[A]ll of the city's essential services and most of its industry were destroyed.... [U]rban life was made almost unbearable by an absence of grain reserves ... and severance of access to agricultural areas by French encirclement.... When the fighting ended [in 1947 with the French retaking Hanoi] people were reluctant to return because of delayed restoration of services, destruction of homes, lack of commerce and cap-ital, exorbitant costs of living and patriotic distaste at the idea of returning to a zone of French control. In 1948–1949, Hanoi's population may have been as low as 10,000 (Turley, 1975).

Among the accounts we have of Hanoi in the difficult interreg-num between the loss of Viet Minh control in early 1947 and the retaking of the city by Ho Chi Minh's forces in 1954, after the battle of Dien Bien Phu, are diaries of Hanoi residents and French documents. These accounts make clear that France, having retaken

31

the city, sought to reintroduce and replicate the French colonial administrative and economic system in Hanoi and as far into surrounding North Vietnam as Vietnamese forces would allow them to penetrate. A large and active French security apparatus was re-energized, utilizing thousands of French and Vietnamese agents in searches for pro-Viet Minh activists. Small business gradually returned to the city, providing an economic base for a rapidly expanding population driven into urban migration by a declining rural economy. This also provided many opportunities for Viet Minh activists to hide and do political work. City services and commercial life were revived, though almost entirely dependent on France. A Communist cadre working among Hanoi's intellectual and cultural figures described the scene in both animated and melancholy terms:

Hang Dao, Hang Ngang, Dong Xuan Market ... they were as they had been, trade was all animated, French and American goods were all available, and there were more hairstylists than before.... I rode back to the North Gate of the Citadel. The scars left by bullets were still there, and I felt stinging pain. The [French] Buoi School had become an automobile collection point for the French army. Every afternoon ... I remembered the poetry of the Truc Bach Lake and Co Ngu Road, with its lines about the red flowering trees, and I was troubled as I recalled a time without worries, when we carried our books to school, that time ten years before when I had gone out with the girlfriend and classmate who would later become my companion for life (Nguyen Bac, 1994).

For Ho Chi Minh's cadres, the return to dangerous underground work in Hanoi during the French occupation between 1947 and 1954 was heady business indeed. The dangers and the thrills of that return from the resistance bases in the mountains north of Hanoi and infiltrating a city held tightly by the French could not be understated.

By mid-1954, when Ho Chi Minh's forces once again retook the city, the population had risen to perhaps 400,000, of whom about 40,000 were 'market stallholders, shopkeepers, pedlars and sidewalk hawkers' (Thrift and Forbes, 1986). At the time Ho Chi Minh's forces defeated the French at Dien Bien Phu in 1954 and the French officials, soldiers, and their families began to flee, Hanoi was a city of victory and hope for many of its citizens. 'I wish you could have seen Hanoi then', an Eastern European diplomat told *New York Times* correspondent Harrison Salisbury in Hanoi in late 1966. 'The city was so lovely. Every building had been painted, the streets were spruced up and there were flowers everywhere' (Salisbury, 1967). French administration had collapsed, and along with that collapse thousands of French officials and business people and their families departed rapidly for France. Nguyen Bac, who worked in Hanoi during the French occupation and kept an extraordinary diary of his experiences, describes the pell-mell departure of the French.

French merchants began to sell their shops, their houses, their belongings. Senior officials and senior civil servants were even more audacious. They also made ready to sell their houses to prepare to go south or go to France. Open air markets sprang up on the sidewalks of Quang Trung Street, down to Tuyen Quang Lake. The fat lady owners, their faces thickly powdered, perched themselves on their salon chairs and sold everything: trunks, beds, carved ebony beds, suits, ties, shoes, high heeled shoes, wardrobes with mirrors, spring beds from Hong Kong, condensers, glasses and cups, antique vases....

People from outside the city and from the provinces came in to buy and carry them back home, at prices so cheap that it was pointless not to buy. Houses were dirt cheap. My wife suggested that we buy a two story house on Ham Long. I rejected that, saying that all cadres must live in collective housing and none in private homes (Nguyen Bac, 1994).

But the Democratic Republic of Vietnam also inherited a poor and crowded capital with little industry and high unemployment, 'cut off from its *raison d'etre*: France' (Thrift and Forbes, 1986). Viet Minh officials marched in to take over city services and government departments to find that key information had disappeared and key personnel, both Vietnamese and French, had fled. In the initial months after Ho's forces re-entered the city in mid-1954, Viet Minh officials worked warily with Vietnamese civil servants who had been under the French system, many of whom were highly anxious at the entrance of the rebels.

In the years after 1954, Hanoi's economic and urban planners were strongly influenced by Soviet and Chinese models of economic planning and urban design. And pride in their traditional capital, now the capital of their socialist state, also prodded political figures and planners on toward traditional socialist modes of industrial development. In the late 1950s industrial development increased more rapidly in Hanoi than in any other North Vietnamese city, as hundreds of private enterprises were merged into state-run and co-operative enterprises (Plate 12) and large new factories were built with Soviet and Chinese aid. Newer factories were often congregated outside the then small central city, but what were considered city suburbs in 1958 became part of the city proper in the late 1980s and early 1990s, causing significant problems of industrial pollution and industrial transfer. And some smaller- and medium-sized factories were situated even within the small, late 1950s city proper, also creating significant pollution, safety, and traffic problems when Hanoi's planners confronted a bustling urban capital of several million after the beginning of *doi moi* (renovation) in 1986 (Turley, 1975; Thrift and Forbes, 1986).

12. Hanoi central department store, 1950s. (Nguyen Hong Sam)

With the division of Vietnam into two regimes, albeit pending elections, the South could no longer be relied upon to feed the North. Northern Vietnamese agriculture was collectivized in the mid- and late 1950s, often with substantial pain and bloodshed, and feeding the cities became a key priority for the northern regime. What then were considered the city's 'suburbs' 'were made the focus of an intensive campaign to increase productivity by planting more vegetables and other staples', a process speeded by strong collectivization and co-operativeness in the Hanoi area (Thrift and Forbes, 1986).

A number of structures in Hanoi bear tribute to the Soviet influence, some built during the 1950s and 1960s and some later. They include the Ho Chi Minh Mausoleum on Ba Dinh Square in central Hanoi (Colour Plate 8), the Ho Chi Minh Museum (Colour Plate 9), the Soviet–Vietnamese Friendship Cultural Palace, and the headquarters of the Hanoi Communist Party and governmental apparatus, as well as much of Hanoi's pre-Vietnam war residential housing stock and industrial facilities (Logan, 1995). The dual focus on industrialization and feeding the city persisted until the early 1960s. But with the onset of hostilities with the United States in the mid-1960s, Hanoi gradually returned to a war footing—factories were reconverted to military use, and agriculture began to feed armies as well as civilian cities (Turley, 1975).

Hanoi during the Vietnam war was a city at war and, for long periods, a city emptied of many of its citizens. Harrison Salisbury (1967), described his arrival in the city in late 1966:

All around I felt the vibrant, pulsating city—traffic on the road, the railroad beside it, the hundreds of bicycles. Every truck seemed to have a canopy of jungle leaves and branches and many of the cyclists had leaves woven into their sun helmets—camouflage. It was the order of the day and of the night.... Camouflage was not confined to trucks and cars. Most North Vietnamese men wore pith sun helmets, women wore broad conical straw hats and schoolchildren wore a heavy plaited straw hat which was said to be almost impervious to shrapnel fragments, and all these headpieces were turned into a kind of bird's nest of leaves and twigs. Even bicycles were camouflaged and babies carried on their mothers' backs were sometimes decked out in leaves.

Between early 1965 and the cessation of Vietnam war in the North in 1973, Hanoi suffered bombing by American forces, more often in the suburban, industrial, and transport areas but at times—especially during the Christmas bombing of 1972—within the inner part of the city and residential neighbourhoods as well. Factories, government offices, universities, and commercial establishments were relocated to the countryside, sometimes close to Hanoi and sometimes much further away. And between early 1965 and late 1968 waves upon waves of citizens, often women and children, were evacuated from Hanoi to live and work in rural villages, creating at times an eerie, childless sense to an otherwise bustling city.

Based on statistics gathered from numerous Vietnamese, French, and other sources, Nigel Thrift and Dean Forbes have estimated that Hanoi's population fell from roughly 900,000 in early 1965 to perhaps 400,000 (mainly government, military, and other personnel) in 1968, when the city was being regularly bombed. The population then increased rapidly until April 1972, when massive re-evacuations began once again after American bombing recommenced. In this phase, perhaps 60 per cent of the city's population was re-evacuated, and Hanoi's population may have fallen from 1.2 million in early 1972 to 0.5 million later that year. And several thousand more people were killed in the American military attacks on Christmas Day 1972 (Turley, 1975; Thrift and Forbes, 1986).

The American bombing, more targeted around the city and toward industrial, military, and transport targets than toward civilian facilities, damaged a number of important historical structures but did not destroy as many as might have been expected. The centre of Hanoi's French colonial railway station was hit by an American bomb in 1972, and repairs possible at the time could not restore the grandeur of the main part of the station. To this day the Hanoi railway station stands as a monument to French colonial architecture, to the Christmas bombing of 1972, and to the Soviet internationalist style of its post-bombing central hall renovation.

When the peace agreement ending the war in the North was signed in 1973, Hanoi's population began streaming back in and some renovation efforts began. Severe housing shortages—caused by bombing damage in many cases—limited return rates and the effective reuse of the city, and it was not until well after the takeover of the South in 1975 and reunification of the country in 1976 that Hanoi's industrial, commercial, service, and educational sectors were running at anything approaching full capacity for that period (Turley, 1975; Thrift and Forbers, 1986).

Hanoi remained a very poor city well into the 1980s. Soviet-style heavy industrialization remained government policy, but there were few funds for investment and little leeway for the private entrepreneurship that had leavened Hanoi's economy in past centuries and decades. An American visitor in the mid-1980s, on the eve of *doi moi*, found a sad and poor city.

There were few street lights and they were very dim. The city was dark, and in the middle of the block where the lights did not reach, it was black. This made walking difficult because of the disrepair of the streets. Cracks, holes, upheaved or sunken bricks made it easy to trip in the dark. In those sections where the street lights did not work, whole blocks would be dark.... But even so, the bicycles streamed by in multitudes. They had no lights; like phantoms they glided out of the darkness to silently brush by and disappear back into the darkness....

The middle of Hanoi was unlike any capital city I knew. No neon lights, no cars parked along the street ... hardly any motorized vehicles, no wailing sirens in the night, no cruising police cars ..., no stores with lit-up window displays, no flashing theater signs, no aircraft overhead (Downs, 1991).

And, just as economic reform began, a senior political leader re-emphasized the depths to which Hanoi had fallen.

It should be honestly and frankly admitted that ... urban life in Hanoi is at its lowest ebb and not commensurate with its position as a capital, and even more so with its people, who are endowed with a very heroic history and glorious traditions. This has saddened not only the people in the capital and the people in the entire country, but also our friends in the world.

Food supply and wage payments are still unstable.... Electricity and water supplies are also at the lowest level and very irregular. Housing, roads and means of transportation are in serious shortage and fraught with difficulties. Public order and security and urban life from streets to population centres, from stores to opera houses, and from schools to hospitals to marketplaces are rapidly deteriorating (Nguyen Thanh Binh, 1988).

But Hanoi had also remained intact. And with the advent of *doi moi* in late 1986, the city came alive once again. Private entrepreneurs reappeared on the streets and set up stalls, commercial and some residential spaces were gradually renovated or spruced up, and traffic increased rapidly. Industrial growth increased rapidly in the suburban areas and, in light industry, well within the city proper. By the early 1990s, there was no longer a concern that Hanoi was fading as a city; instead, the anxiety was that Hanoi was developing too rapidly, its quiet life and its charms—as well as its colonial and pre-colonial architecture—endangered by the new market economy.

In the 1990s, Hanoi is a city of renewed economic and cultural vitality for many of its citizens. Light industrial production, service industries, and other economic sectors have been rapidly improving, and private entrepreneurship—including government officials who often hold second and third jobs in addition to the civil service employment—has financed improvements to the supply of houses and increased consumption and savings. And Hanoi has benefited from the Vietnamese economic reforms much more quickly than many residents of rural areas and smaller cities.

Even within Hanoi, the new market economy has not, of course, benefited all of Hanoi's residents equally. Wealth has come to some, evoked by luxurious multi-storey houses on the West Lake, new cars and motorcycles, expensive night-life, and other increased consumption, while others among Hanoi's people remain mired in poverty. A Vietnamese poet evoked both the celebration of Hanoi's new life and the intense pain of its less fortunate residents in a 1992 poem entitled 'New Year's Fireworks'.

The whole city seems to explode.
Fireworks thunder in the distance.
An old man with a stick and bag
sobs quietly by the train station.

The whole city seems to be on fire.
The sky suddenly streaked with flares.

A woman picks through the garbage,
shrivels up under a bridge.

The whole city seems awash in smoke.
The smell of fires fills the sky.
A streetwalker greets the New Year
alone beneath a tree.

The whole city seems to crack open.
Firecrackers cover the pavements.
A child survives alone in the dust,
curls up under a verandah listening.

Smoke rises, explosions rumble.
What battle has just passed through?
A man on a wooden crutch sits by the river.
He dreams of home—

(Nguyen Duy, 1995)

As an economically vibrant Hanoi entered the 1990s, policy concerns turned toward reducing substantial youth unemployment, improving city services and—perhaps in contradiction to other economic goals—preserving traditional structures (Plate 13) and neighbourhoods of Hanoi, particularly in the central area that a United Nations specialist termed 'a jewel of an architectural ensemble' (Khan, 1994). Of special concern were the older Chinese, French, and French–Vietnamese structures and boulevards in the central city, as well as the old quarter north of Hoan Kiem Lake, in the northern part of the central city.

Since the early 1990s a number of plans to preserve central areas of Hanoi and the old quarter have been formulated by Hanoi and central government officials, as well as by foreign specialists recruited by the United Nations and other international groups to work with Vietnamese officials. But an understanding of the potential and the frustrations of these attempts to guide the development of, and to conserve and preserve, a beautiful Asian capital, that until recently had moved more slowly to destroy its past than many other Asian capitals, must take into account a context of centuries of attempts to plan the development of Hanoi.

As we have seen, planning for the development of Hanoi has

13. Early view of Hanoi Cathedral. (Nguyen Hong Sam)

been a preoccupation of Vietnam's rulers, domestic and foreign. Emperors built or reduced Thang Long depending on their priorities and visions for the capital, and its relative importance in their plans for their empires. The French planned and built as a colonial power. Soviet architectural and planning advisers sought to mould Hanoi, or at least key buildings, along a style that they wished to

1. Remnants of the old Citadel at Co Loa still visible in the city. (Nguyen Huy Kham)

2. Outer view of Van Mieu (Temple of Literature), original site of
   Vietnam's imperial university. (Nguyen Huy Kham)

3. The Army Museum, located on the outskirts of the old Citadel and beside the Flag Tower. (Nguyen Huy Kham)

4. Fine Arts Museum, constructed during the French period. (Nguyen Huy Kham)

5. Hanoi Opera House, constructed by the French and opened in 1911, a conscious imitation of the Paris Opera House and a key site during the 1945 revolution. (Nguyen Huy Kham)

6. Soviet–Vietnamese Friendship Cultural Palace, built on the site of the former French Exposition Hall in downtown Hanoi. (Nguyen Huy Kham)

7. History Museum, by the Red River in eastern central Hanoi. (Nguyen Huy Kham)

8. Ho Chi Minh Mausoleum on Ba Dinh Square. (Nguyen Huy Kham)

9. Ho Chi Minh Museum, constructed with Soviet assistance and located near Ba Dinh Square. (Nguyen Huy Kham)

10. Economic reform has brought new bustle and pressures to Ma May Street in central Hanoi. (Nguyen Huy Kham)

11. Quan Thanh Pagoda (Nguyen Huy Kham)

12. One Pillar Pagoda, a key symbol of modern Hanoi, located near Ba Dinh Square between the Ho Chi Minh Mausoleum and the Ho Chi Minh Museum. (Nguyen Huy Kham)

13. Quan Su Pagoda, originally site of a guest-house for foreign envoys, and still a religious centre for Vietnamese Buddhism. (Nguyen Huy Kham)

14. Quan Chuong Gate, one of the gates to the earlier Thang Long city. (Nguyen Huy Kham)

15. North Gate to the old Hanoi Citadel, another of the early city gates. (Nguyen Huy Kham)

16. Flag Tower within the former Citadel (now the Ministry of Defence) and overlooking central Hanoi. (Nguyen Huy Kham)

17. Hoan Kiem Lake in central Hanoi, a central cultural and political symbol of Hanoi's place in a unified Vietnam. (Nguyen Huy Kham)

18. Hoa Phong Tower in central Hanoi. (Nguyen Huy Kham)

19. The Presidential Palace, originally built for the French Governor-General, now used to receive important foreign visitors. In its garden is Ho Chi Minh's former residence, the house built on stilts. (Nguyen Huy Kham)

20. Hanoi Cathedral, formerly the St. Joseph's Cathedral, opened on Christmas Day 1886. (Nguyen Huy Kham)

21. The National Library, formerly the Pierre Pasquier Library, in French Beaux Arts style, completed in 1919. (Nguyen Huy Kham)

22. Ho Chi Minh's house on stilts, located in the garden of the former French Governor General's Palace and a striking counterpoint to the Ho Chi Minh Mausoleum located just south-east. (Nguyen Huy Kham)

make common among the Soviet Union and its allies. Particularly when we reach back to imperial times, a policy of developing and expanding Hanoi was a feature of imperial rule when emperors viewed Thang Long as their appropriate capital for a proud nation. Why should that be any different in the 1990s?

And that is the conundrum of planning for Hanoi. Vietnam emerges from its wars with China, France, and the United States, from its submission to the Soviet Union, and from decades of desultory central planning into an era of political independence and economic revitalization determined to show her vitality and her central role as the capital of a reunified Vietnam. Limiting the development of a proud capital city by a proud regime under such circumstances is difficult policy indeed. But regulating change so that sustainable development is facilitated, while difficult, may be possible (Logan, 1995b). And conservation and preservation go far beyond the physical realities of construction; as Graham Brookes (1994) has put it, 'the challenge for Hanoi is more about the totality of the conservation of a living organism than the repair of decayed building fabric'. A prominent Vietnamese architect and planner put it more even more forcefully in late 1993: 'We have not so far come to an agreement in viewpoint, and there is not yet a comprehensive policy for heritage conservation, nor effective measures. A lot of breaches are still happening. We complain a lot, but there is no plan for action. The alarm has gone off for so long, but who has the main responsibility and authority?' (Dam Trong Phuong, 1993).

In the socialist era there have been a number of attempts to plan the development of urban and rural Hanoi. The first such effort focused more on economic planning for Hanoi rather than urban planning *per se*, and we have described that in some detail earlier: the late 1950s and early 1960s' focus on industrializing Hanoi, strengthening collectivized and co-operative agriculture on the outskirts of the city, and the reorganization of city administration down to the district and block level (Turley, 1975; Thrift and Forbes, 1986). A more specific urban plan termed the 'Zone plan for Hanoi construction' was developed in the late 1950s, publicly exhibited in 1960, and, according to William Logan, seems to

41

have been adopted by the government in 1965. Under the zone plan, the old city (thirty-six streets) was to have been commercially revitalized and new development centred to the west of the West Lake, south-west of the city, and across the Red River to the east in Gia Lam. The railway network was to have been strengthened, and additional bridges built across the Red River. With the onset of war in the North no significant parts of the zone plan were implemented, but, as Logan notes, 'it set a pattern for later plans, notably in seeing expansion of the commercial centre around [the West Lake]' (Logan, 1995a).

In the early 1970s, just before the war wound down, Soviet planners once again assisted vigorously in the development of a new urban plan for Hanoi. The new Soviet–Vietnamese plan called for intensive development of a new city centre near the West Lake, a major highway through the old quarter of the city, and discrete residential and industrial developments to the west, south-west, and east of the city. Logan (1995a), who has studied these efforts in a more detailed fashion than any other Western scholar, calls the results 'fantastic, being based on a poor understanding of Hanoi's history and demography and totally divorced from both the local culture and the economic realities of an impoverished government'.

In the 1990s, a number of plans have been proposed by Vietnamese institutions and by foreign advisors. Many of these plans sought to enhance the economic value of the French villas and the old quarter (Plate 14) by returning them to economic usage, along with severe constraints on changes to the structures and new construction (Hoang Huu Phe and Nishimura, 1992; Logan 1994 and 1995b; Gillespie and Logan, 1995; Khan, 1995).

One of the first of such plans focused in a more limited fashion on the old quarter rather than, in Soviet style, on master planning for all of Hanoi. In 1990 a team from the Asian Institute of Technology (AIT) in Bangkok sought to map and classify the old quarter and to propose a series of preservation and conservation measures, as well as realistic constraints on the implementation of such a plan. While the AIT plan was not implemented, the team's 1990 study of the area including its detailed research on the layout of the place and the structure of its buildings remains an important

14. Hanoi market street, 1910. (Nguyen Hong Sam)

source of information on the ancient quarter of Hanoi (Hoang Huu Phe and Nishimura, 1992).

Another plan, in which Vietnamese officials collaborated with the United Nations Educational, Scientific, and Cultural Organization (Unesco) (which in turn fielded Logan as expert consultant) in the early 1990s, proposed a five-phase project aimed at identifying, classifying, and documenting Hanoi's old quarter (including both the thirty-six streets and the French quarter); developing legislation, policies, and guidelines to protect the older areas of the city; developing implementation structures and systems; carrying out extensive public relations activities; and evaluation and follow-up discussions (Logan 1994 and 1995; Gillespie and Logan, 1995).

A second effort was initiated by Australian investors concerned about the threats to the architectural heritage of Hanoi. Formed as the Friends of Hanoi Architectural Heritage International Foundation in early 1993, run by a joint group of Australians and Vietnamese, the group sought to publicize the dangers to Hanoi's architectural and urban fabric and to field pilot projects in the old quarter, the French quarter, and other older areas of Hanoi. The Foundation sought to emphasize the economic benefits of

43

conservation and the need for integrated approaches to conservation and development in Hanoi. 'It is absolutely not an architectural problem which faces Hanoi', noted an Australian founder of the preservation group in late 1993, '[but] a management problem which needs to draw on an immense range of skills: architects, town planners, interior designers, civil engineers, statisticians, land managers, lawyers' (Hoggard, 1993).

In nearly four years of activity, before the activities of the Foundation were turned over to Vietnamese counterparts at the end of 1996, the Foundation sponsored two 'Friends' weeks' to celebrate Hanoi's heritage and advocate preservation and sustainable development by building public awareness, held a symposium on 'Developing while preserving Hanoi', in November 1993, conducted a pilot project to renovate the Cau Dong Pagoda, and compiled a database of historically significant structures and other conditions and events.

In late 1994, the Office of the Chief Architect of Hanoi received $1.8 million in aid from the Australian government to produce a development plan and planning ordinances for Hanoi, a local structure plan for the main part of central Hanoi, and an ancient city conservation strategy for the protection and appropriate development of the old quarter. A number of other government and foreign institutions were involved in this planning project as well. A plan approved by central and municipal authorities in 1995 under the planning strategy funded by the Australian government sought to secure the boundaries of the old quarter, halt the demolition of landmarked sites, and limit the height of new construction to 16 metres. Implementation, however, remained the key problem (Logan, 1994 and 1995b; Gillespie and Logan, 1995; Karr, 1995).

In their own legislative process, Hanoi government officials have sought to discourage the construction of high towers and high density residential and office space in the central city, and to encourage residential, commercial, and industrial construction, as well as relocation, in suburbs and satellite areas. In 1993 municipal regulations sought to limit construction in the old quarter to three stories, restrict motorized vehicle traffic, and encourage commercial development based on 'traditional and national art and handicraft activities as well as cultural and tourist services' (Hanoi People's Committee, 1993). A Hoan Kiem master plan unveiled in 1994 also sought to limit building height. And in the spring of 1995, in a stern response to related pressures, the Prime Minister and the Hanoi city government ordered the razing of more than 150 houses and other structures that had been illegally constructed on the dike system outside Hanoi that protects the city from the traditional ravages of the Red River.

Each of these measures has met with some success and, at times, failure as well, given the significant economic pressure on Hanoi's central city area (Colour Plate 10) and the old quarter and, in an era of economic liberalization, less control by city and central government officials over the use of land and buildings than in the past. Property speculation was rampant in Hanoi from the late 1980s to the mid-1990s, and much construction was completed without appropriate city permits. High-rise office and residential structures were under construction on the site of the former Hoa Lo prison, which had kept Vietnamese prisoners and later Americans (who dubbed it the Hanoi Hilton), and at a number of other central city sites. But by the mid-1990s, several pilot conservation projects were underway, including a heritage list of particularly important structures, and supported by the Friends of Hanoi Architectural Heritage International Foundation. A Hanoi master plan through the year 2010, which obtained government approval in 1993, focused on the preservation of the ancient quarter (Logan, 1994 and 1995b; Gillespie and Logan, 1995).

Special efforts were focused on the ancient quarter for its significant historical and cultural importance. The premier Vietnamese historian of Hanoi, Nguyen Vinh Phuc, put it bluntly: 'In the next five years if we are unable to preserve the old streets, we will have failed future generations. The next years are crucial if we are to succeed.' And a young official expressed the commitment of his generation to preserving Hanoi as a symbol of Vietnamese perseverance, rebellion, and development in the face of economic and policy challenges: 'What you see in Hanoi isn't French architectural heritage, but ... our heritage. It's our beautiful city unless we destroy it' (Johnson, 1996).

4
Traces of Old Thang Long in the New Hanoi

MORE remains of old Hanoi than many other ancient Asian cities. Despite the effects of wars with China, France, and the United States, traces of old Hanoi are readily visible for visitors to the new Hanoi, almost always in the midst of the development since the Vietnamese policies of economic reform adopted in late 1986.

Perhaps the most important traces of the past in present-day Hanoi are in the social fabric of the city rather than in individual structures. The old city (the thirty-six streets area) retains its bustling and commercial sensibility. The French quarter built by Paul Bert, Ernest Hebrard, and their colleagues remains, for the most part, an area of broad leafy boulevards and imposing neo-classical and mixed French/Indo-Chinese-style buildings, interspersed with smaller, still leafy streets lined with French-style villas, refurbished or decaying, sitting proudly through the decades. Some traditional, low-rise Chinese-style areas remain as well (Plate 15), one storey buildings and complexes marked every so often by small ornate gates, many with the Chinese-style characters still visible. Hanoi remains a city best learned and appreciated by walking, perhaps the only Asian capital that can still be strolled pleasantly from end to urban end.

Among the many traces of the old Hanoi still visible (and in most cases accessible) are the following sites, chosen for their historical importance and architectural value from the many other hundreds of buildings and sites remaining from the city's complex but still present past.

15. Chinese-style area of Hanoi, early twentieth century. (Nguyen Hong Sam)

Hanoi's Ancient Sites

Co Loa Citadel

The earliest traces of Hanoi still extant are outside the current central city, about 18 kilometres to the west, where the remnants of the early citadel of Co Loa may be found. Co Loa was built in the third century BC as the capital of Emperor An Duong Vuong's empire of Au Lac. Sometimes termed Vietnam's first capital, Co Loa is celebrated as a fortress of resistance against northern aggression. Over the years Co Loa has also been a rich archaeological site, yielding bronze objects and farming and household implements that go back over 2,000 years. Originally a fortified palace, the ruins are still surrounded by the remains of earthen walls, a moat, and remnants of watch towers.

Co Loa is little visited by the Vietnamese or by foreigners (other than in early January, when an important festival is held to honour the Emperor who built it), but it remains an important Vietnamese

47

architectural and historical site, Still visible, though in most cases heavily reconstructed, are the gate to Co Loa's inner citadel, remnants of the imperial palace, and several temples. The An Duong Vuong Temple contains a bronze statue of the Emperor of that name (Nguyen Vinh Phuc, 1995).

Pre-colonial Pagodas and Temples

Among the earliest traces of old Thang Long still visible today are pagodas, temples, and other heavily Chinese-influenced remnants of pre-colonial Hanoi life. Some of these pagodas and temples have been extensively and repeatedly restored, and almost all look at least somewhat different from their appearance in centuries past, but they remain remarkably evocative of the centuries before the French arrived. One of the oldest is the Tran Quoc Pagoda, built 1,400 years ago under Emperor Ly Nam De. The pagoda now stands at Ca Vang (Goldfish) Islet, near the West Lake, in the midst of busy restaurants, food markets, and boats.

Another example is the Quan Thanh Pagoda on Quan Thanh Street, originally built in the eleventh century to honour a mythical genie that had slayed a serpent (Colour Plate 11). The pagoda has been substantially renovated thereafter. A bronze statue of the genie stands inside, its feet rubbed to a burnish by worshippers.

A further example is the Chua Mot Cot (One Pillar Pagoda), which stands just in front of the Ho Chi Minh Museum and south of the Ho Chi Minh Mausoleum, next to the smaller but also important Dien Huu Pagoda. Also built in the eleventh century, the Chua Mot Cot is a wooden structure built on a stone pillar in a lotus pond. The Chua Mot Cot has been repeatedly destroyed and repeatedly restored, including a recent restoration in the mid-1950s after the pagoda was destroyed by the French. Perhaps because of that history with the French, the pagoda has become a common artistic and political symbol for Vietnam and its people (Colour Plate 12).

The Van Mieu (Temple of Literature), also constructed in the eleventh century as a Confucian pagoda, housed Vietnam's first imperial university, the Quoc Tu Giam. Stelae recalling the names of the graduates of Vietnam's fiercely competitive imperial examinations still stand (Plate 16). The Van Mieu is one of Hanoi's most well cared for ancient sites, a testimony to the importance of education both in present-day Vietnam and through the centuries. In the early 1990s the stelae bearing the names of the laureates from the eighty-two imperial examinations held between 1484 and 1779

16. Chinese stelae near Hanoi, 1929. (Nguyen Hong Sam)

49

were covered by structures donated by the American Express firm, an early example of foreign corporate philanthropy in Vietnam that attempts to preserve ancient Vietnamese sites.

A number of other important sites also bear witness to pre-colonial Hanoi and its preservation (along with substantial restoration and renovation) down the centuries. In the north-west part of the city still stands the Voi Phuc (Temple of the Kneeling Elephants), built in the eleventh century to honour an imperial prince who defended Vietnamese territory against Chinese invaders using a band of elephants. On Quan Su Street in central Hanoi stands the often reconstructed Quan Su Pagoda (Ambassadors Pagoda), situated on the location of a guest-house for visiting foreign envoys in the seventeenth century, and still a working and training centre for Vietnamese Buddhism (Colour Plate 13). On the east side of the West Lake stands the Kim Lien Pagoda, still home to Buddhist nuns and which houses a statue of the benefactor who restored the temple in 1792.

In a more prosaic vein, downtown Hanoi (near Dang Tien Dong and Nguyen Luong Bang streets) is also the site of the Dong Da Mound, the remaining burial ground for invaders defeated by Emperor Quang Trung during Tet in 1789. A pagoda stands at the top of the mound, on which banyan trees also grow. And the Hai Ba Trung Temple, also in central Hanoi at Tho Lao and Dong Nhan streets, honours the Trung sisters, legendary historical figures, for their revolt against and defeat of northern invaders some 1,950 years ago. Many other ancient pagodas and temples, substantially restored and rebuilt, dot other areas of Hanoi as well, interspersed in charming ways with private residences, schools, hospitals, and workplaces.

Gates to the Royal and the Commoners' cities were an important feature of early Hanoi, but few traces remain of them today. Two gates still visible are the North Gate of the Hanoi Citadel, discussed briefly below, and the Quang Chuong Gate, originally one of a series of entrances to the earthworks around the former Thang Long city. Built in 1817, the Quang Chuong Gate is now located on Hang Chieu Street in the northern part of the city (Colour Plate 14). Historian Nguyen Vinh Phuc describes it: 'Above the main entrance is a watch tower ... a gazebo-like structure which formerly was occupied by security guards throughout the day and night. On the left side there is a stele sculpted in 1882 on the order of ... Hoang Dieu prohibiting soldiers from embarrassing funeral processions through the gate' (Nguyen Vinh Phuc, 1995).

The Hanoi Citadel

The great Hanoi Citadel, first built in the sixteenth and seventeenth centuries as Vietnam's imperial city and rebuilt in the early eighteenth century as the home of the Nguyen Dynasty, is the crowning architectural achievement of early modern Vietnam. Much of the Citadel was destroyed by the French in the 1880s, and the scars of cannon balls fired by the French in April 1882 remain on the Citadel's North Gate (Colour Plate 15). The other gates no longer stand.

Of the many buildings within the Citadel, the hexagonal Cot Co (Flag Tower), built in 1812, remains extant. The French military occupiers used its impressive height for observations and communications. This helps to account for its survival. The Cot Co is an important political and cultural symbol for Vietnam, of Hanoi, and of the Vietnamese military. The tower itself is built on three overlapping square bases. Within the tower is a low and narrow spiral staircase that can be climbed to the top; given the still low height of Hanoi's townscape, the view from 60 metres height is still an impressive sight. Flower and fan-shaped holes provide light to the tower's interior (Colour Plate 16). The Cot Co also accords excellent views of the areas within the still-restricted Citadel site, now the home of Vietnam's secretive Ministry of Defence. The only better view of the Citadel's internal area, rarely seen by foreign visitors, is from reconnaissance aircraft. Many Vietnamese citizens have never been inside the old Citadel area.

Hoan Kiem Lake

Hoan Kiem Lake (Lake of the Returned Sword), the spiritual and cultural centre of Hanoi, recalls the myth of Emperor Ly Thai To, who used a magical sword given to him by a divine tortoise to resist Chinese occupation in the fifteenth century. As the legend goes, after defeating the northern enemy the Emperor sailed to the centre of the lake to return the sword to the tortoise.

A small structure, the Thap Rua (Tortoise Tower) is situated on a small island in the middle of the lake. And on a small islet on the north-east side of the lake stands the Ngoc Son Temple, which memorializes the Vietnamese national hero Tran Hung Dao. The successor to earlier pavilions and pagodas, the current temple was built in the nineteenth century by a Vietnamese intellectual and writer. The tower is named Thap But (Pen Brush Tower), and on it is marked an inscription that relates to Vietnamese writers—'write on the blue sky'. Originally an early Vietnamese naval training site, Hoan Kiem Lake is graced by ancient trees, the temple, several old structures, walking paths, and benches (Colour Plate 17; Plate 17). On pleasant evenings hundreds if not thousands of Hanoi residents stroll around this landmark, and in the mornings many exercise beside it (Colour Plate 18).

17. Looking off Hoan Kiem Lake. (Nguyen Hong Sam)

Ba Dinh Square

Although heavily influenced by French construction and later by Soviet architecture, Ba Dinh Square, the political centre of Hanoi, was in ancient times close to the site of the west gate of the Hanoi Citadel. Converted by the French into a garden and then into a square, it was here that Ho Chi Minh's forces gathered with Hanoi's citizens on 2 September 1945 to declare the independence of the Democratic Republic of Vietnam.

Ba Dinh Square is carefully maintained as a political symbol. The northern edge of the square is dominated by the former élite Lycee Albert Serraut, now the headquarters of the Central Committee of the Vietnamese Communist Party. The General Secretary of the Party and other high-ranking Party officials meet foreign guests in the Lycee's reception rooms.

At the north-west corner of the square stands the Palace of the French Governor-General, completed in 1902, and further west the botanical gardens within the Governor-General's compound, where Ho Chi Minh's house on stilts was built after he refused to live in the Palace. As of mid-1997, Vietnam's former Prime Minister, Pham Van Dong, still lived within these gardens. On the west side of the square is the Ho Chi Minh Mausoleum, jointly designed by Vietnamese and Russian architects. Further south-west, through the trees, lies the Ho Chi Minh Museum.

On the south side of the square stands a yellow French-style villa that at mid-1997 housed offices for then Deputy Prime Minister Pham Van Khai. In the south-west corner of the square is the Indo-Chinese-styled French Financial Service headquarters which now house Vietnam's Ministry of Foreign Affairs. This building was constructed during the Hebrard era when local influences were brought into French colonial architecture. To the east of the square, directly across the Ho Chi Minh Mausoleum, is Vietnam's monument to its fallen soldiers. And slightly north-east is the defiantly Russian-style National Assembly building, erected during the 1970s and one of the few undistinguished structures on the square. Finally in the north-east corner of the square, behind a discreet fence, sits the Ba Dinh Club, formerly a French recreation facility and now serving as a gathering place for retired senior Party and government officials and Party members of long service.

The Thirty-six Streets

Hanoi's famed ancient quarter, originally a major part of the Commoners' City in imperial times and a source of artisan goods for the court, has survived Chinese invasion, French colonization, and American bombing but is now under stress from the resurgence of a market economy. The ancient quarter is a source of great pride to Hanoi's residents and to many other Vietnamese, for with the enormous changes to other parts of the city, especially during the French colonial era, it is sometimes said that 'the soul of old Hanoi ... took refuge in the traditional quarter' (Do Xuan Sang, 1977) (Plate 18).

Located north of the Hoan Kiem Lake near a bend in the Red River, the thirty-six streets (thirty-six *pho phuong*), originally Ke Cho (market town), were initially guild and artisan neighbour-hoods. The streets bear the names—silk, salt, paper, jewellery, bamboo baskets, dyers, silversmiths—of the artisan groups that originally worked on them or goods originally sold here. Communal houses or temples based in particular local groups or guilds also dot the ancient quarter. In recent years preservation efforts in Hanoi have focused on this neighbourhood, where economic and population pressures are threatening the ancient shops and residences.

Relatively few of the residents of the ancient quarter appear to derive most of their income from artisan activities within the area. In many cases most members of a family living within the quarter may work outside the area in government, service, industrial, or other sectors, while one or two family members maintain a shop within the quarter, either abutting the home (as in a tube house) or separately situated. But the market nature of the old streets remains, crowded from early in the morning until well past dark with traders, merchants, and shopkeepers engaged in transactions of every description.

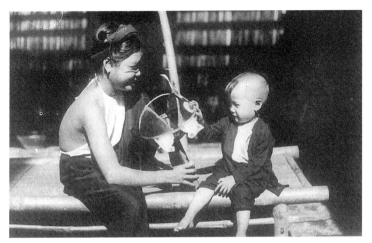

18. Early scene of Tet in the thirty-six streets area of Hanoi. (Nguyen
    Hong Sam)

Peculiar to the area are the famed 'tube houses' of Hanoi, long
and narrow residences fronted by a shop facing the street. The lay-
out of the 'tube houses', which are usually only 2 to 4 metres wide
and two stories tall, has the shop at the front portion, the rooms
containing manufacturing or assembly facilities in the middle, and
the residential and dining quarters at the back. Many 'tube houses'
were originally punctuated by small inner courtyards, with some
having water pools and fountains.

Within the thirty-six streets' area are pagodas, temples, and
other historical sites. They include a number of temples and gathering houses that served as centres for people from other areas of
Vietnam who were living or trading in Hanoi. The Hoa Loc
temple, at 90 Hang Dao Street, for example, originally served a
local group from Hai Hung province in northern Vietnam. Tu Dinh
Thi temple, on Ngo Yen Thai, honours an earlier exponent of
embroidery from Ha Tay province.

A recent historical site is situated on one small street in the old
quarter. At 48 Hang Ngang stands the small house where Ho Chi
Minh drafted Vietnam's 1945 Declaration of Independence. The

ground floor houses a small museum, gradually being taken over by a gift shop, while the second floor remains preserved, at least according to the museum officials, as Ho lived there in 1945 after entering Hanoi from the northern mountains (Hoang Huu Phe and Nishimura, 1990; Matics, 1994; Khan, 1995).

Traces of French Influence in the New Hanoi

Despite war, revolutionary change, and the ravages of time, a number of important French colonial structures remain in the city. For the most part the French did not destroy the edifices they constructed as they withdrew from Hanoi in 1945 and 1954, and for the most part the United States did not target inner-city non-military buildings. But the Hanoi Railway Station bears silent witness to the Christmas Day bombing of 1972, its French structure intact except for the central section, renovated in Soviet style after the bombing.

The imposing former residence of the French Governor-General on Ba Dinh Square houses the offices and reception halls of Vietnam's President and Vice President (Colour Plate 19). Directly beside the Governor-General's residence is the former Lycee Albert Serraut, one of the élite French educational institutions of colonial Hanoi. The main building of the Lycee houses offices and reception rooms for the Central Committeee of the Vietnamese Communist Party. The formerly resplendent villas behind the Lycee, on Phan Dinh Phung street, house senior government and Communist Party officials, including (at mid-1997) Vietnam's Prime Minister.

A number of other important French colonial structures remain in use, some dedicated to their original purposes and others with changed missions. The Opera House, built in 1911 as one of the premiere edifices of colonial France in imitation of the Paris Opera House, is undergoing full renovation in the mid-1990s for the first time in many decades. It remains dedicated to artistic performances and stands as a monument to the construction of a French colonial presence through architecture in the late nineteenth and early twentieth centuries. The former L'École Française d'Extrême Orient (Plate 19), the primary French research centre specializing

19. L'École Française d'Extrême Orient when built. (Nguyen Hong Sam)

in Indo-China, located on Pham Ngu Lao Street, presently houses the Vietnam History Museum (Bao Tang Lich Su). Earlier, it served as a place for exhibiting archaeological finds from around South-East Asia and contained research facilities; it now houses a continuous exhibit narrating Vietnamese history from the Stone Age through the twentieth century.

The former St Joseph's Cathedral, opened on Christmas 1886 after the Bao Thien Pagoda was torn down to make way for the church's construction, remains in use as a Catholic cathedral, though now under Vietnamese control. The name St Joseph's is gone, and today the church is known simply as Nha Tho Lon or Hanoi Cathedral (Colour Plate 20). A number of other French-built Catholic and Protestant churches survive in Hanoi, besides the ruins of others.

The former Maison Centrale (Central Prison), later the Hoa Lo Prison and dubbed the 'Hanoi Hilton' by American prisoners of war, housed imprisoned Vietnamese revolutionaries—including some who are now among Vietnam's most senior leaders—before it held imprisoned Americans. Part of the prison will remain while the rest will give way to a multi-storey residential and office development which is being built on the same site.

The former French appellate court, on Ly Thuong Kiet Street, houses Vietnam's Supreme People's Court. An imposing, if somewhat theoretic, monument to the rule of law as practised under French colonialism and Vietnamese socialism, the building is presently under renovation. Important trials are still held in the ornate, solemn, but fading main courtroom.

The first, and for many decades the only bridge over the Red River, was the Paul Doumer Bridge constructed in 1902. During the Vietnam war the Doumer Bridge was repeatedly bombed by the Americans and just as repeatedly repaired by the Vietnamese. The old Beaux Arts railway station was also constructed by the French, but, as William Logan (1995a) indicates, the station 'reflects [a] break between the Beaux-Arts and the [Soviet] Modern International styles [because of] replacement of the central pavilion after its destruction in an American bombing raid'.

Among the earliest of the French structures, built when military barracks and warehouses were the priority of French construction in its early colonial days, is the former residence and headquarters of the Chief of the General Staff of the French Army on Pham Ngu Lao Street. Now the central building in a complex that houses the Ministry of Defence and Army guest-houses, the military residence and headquarters has had the construction date, 1874–7, carefully preserved on the face of the building over many decades. Vietnamese political and military officials held talks with US Secretary of State Henry Kissinger here in the early 1970s, and the military retains control of the site as a conference and meeting centre.

The Pierre Pasquier Library, also constructed by the French in the Beaux Arts style in 1919, remains Vietnam's National Library (Colour Plate 21). This and the national archives were originally constructed on the grounds of the imperial Vietnamese examination centre, where young scholars once took the imperial examinations as a prerequisite to being named as officials.

Other important French buildings include the original site of Hanoi University, on Le Thanh Tong Street; the imposing Yunnan

Railways Company at Tran Hung Dao and Quan Su streets, opposite the original site of the Hanoi Exposition now the headquarters of the Central Trade Union and the Ministry of Communications; the residence of the French Resident Superior for northern Vietnam, on Ngo Quyen Street near the French-constructed Metropole Hotel, renovated in the early 1990s; and the former headquarters of the French Financial Service, presently the Vietnamese Ministry of Foreign Affairs. Even Hanoi's primary stadium, the Hang Day arena, undergoing renovation in the mid-1990s, was originally the stadium of the Societe d'Education Physique du Tonkin (SEPTO), the French private sports and physical training institution in Hanoi (Wright, 1991; Nguyen Vinh Phuc, 1995).

Not all French colonial buildings were exceptional edifices (Plate 20). French villas dot the city in art deco and other styles, some more distinguished than others, many in a state of faded splendour. And some buildings have fallen prey even to those who remark on the importance of conserving and preserving Hanoi's heritage. One unfortunate example involves the United States. Up until 1954, the US consulate occupied two French-era villas in a

20. French designed police station off Hoan Kiem Lake. (Nguyen Hong Sam)

compound at 22–4 Hai Ba Trung Street in central Hanoi. Over the next forty years that compound and the villas were used as the headquarters for the Vietnam Fatherland Front, a Party-led umbrella group of intellectuals, religious, and cultural organizations. When diplomatic relations between Vietnam and the United States were normalized in the summer of 1995, the compound and the French villas were given back to the US government, which promptly and without public announcement arranged for the demolition of the two villas and turned the grounds into a soccer field and basketball court, pending construction of a new US diplomatic facility. When foreign residents of Hanoi complained to the Vietnamese Foreign Ministry, officials indicated that they had no power over these decisions. 'We know that the preservation of Hanoi is important, and the foreigners keep telling us that as well', said one senior official, 'but these are now U.S. property once again and there is nothing we can do.'

Traces of Soviet Influence in Modern Hanoi

Soviet influence on Hanoi is visible in the undistinguished residential blocks and factory complexes, large and small. More distinguished, or at least prominent, representations of Soviet architectural realism include a number of structures that are important Hanoi landmarks such as the National Assembly building on Ba Dinh Square and the Soviet–Vietnamese Cultural Palace.

The Ho Chi Minh Mausoleum

The Vietnamese stress their role in the design of Ho Chi Minh's final resting place, but Soviet influence is unmistakable. The Mausoleum was designed with substantial Soviet assistance and opened on 2 September 1975, six years after Ho's death. The Mausoleum, like Hoan Kiem Lake and the Chua Mot Cot, are among the government's most important visual symbols of Vietnam. The prominent Vietnamese architectural historian Dang Thai Hoang has called the design and building of the Mausoleum 'an architectural event of important political significance not only to the capital Hanoi but also the whole country' (Dang Thai Hoang, quoted in Logan, 1995a, retranslated).

The Mausoleum is located on the western edge of Ba Dinh Square, on the site where Ho Chi Minh declared the independence of the Democratic Republic of Vietnam in September 1945 (see Colour Plate 8). The Mausoleum was built to house President Ho's mortal remains despite his clearly expressed wishes to be cremated and his ashes scattered. The process by which the Mausoleum came to be designed and constructed was not an easy one. Logan has described the conflict between Soviet designers and Vietnamese architects, led by Mausoleum chief architect Nguyen Ngoc Chan:

The Russians assumed they had the expertise and ventured to lecture the Vietnamese on what made good 'national architecture': 'it must be majestic, symmetrical and solemn'. The Vietnamese appeared to cede to the Russians' superior experience; in fact they quietly but stubbornly stuck to their own ideas, believing that the monument had to fit the Vietnamese Communist Party's guiding principles—'modern, cultured, dignified and simple'. Eventually [Nguyen Ngoc] Chan's original plan prevailed with minor concessions to keep the Russians happy (Logan, 1995a).

The Ho Chi Minh House on Stilts

There is no Soviet influence in the Ho Chi Minh house on stilts, Ho's residence in Hanoi from the late 1950s until his death in 1969. But its warmth and its natural blending into the garden of the French Governor-General's Palace represents such a sharp contrast to the Soviet cold marble and symmetrical design of the Ho Chi Minh Mausoleum in front of it that the Ho residence is discussed here (Tai, 1995). The residence is a warm, informal wooden house on wooden pilings incorporating Vietnamese traditional design elements, created (according to one of the many Ho legends) with Ho's direct input and realized by Vietnamese architects and builders without external assistance.

The house is situated in a lovely garden setting, surrounded by trees and plants, facing the stone-walled lake (Colour Plate 22). Underneath the house, among the wooden pilings, is a rectangular table around which the Political Bureau of the Vietnamese Communist Party and other senior Party and government officials would meet with Ho. Upstairs are a small study and a small bedroom, each still looking the same as when Ho lived and worked here.

Hue-Tam Ho Tai of Harvard University has described the fierce contrast between Ho Chi Minh's warm garden home in life and his cold, marble habitation in death. 'There can be no greater contrast', concludes Tai, 'than between the garden house and the mausoleum. One, devoid of Ho's physical presence, more nearly recalls the man; the other, though built to display Ho's mortal remains, is deadening inside and out' (Tai, 1995).

The Ho Chi Minh Museum

The Ho Chi Minh Museum, located near the Ho Chi Minh Mausoleum, was also built with extensive Soviet as well as Czech assistance, although Vietnamese authorities describe it as a lotus flower reflecting the national culture (see Colour Plate 9). The round, five-storey building exerts a more modern sense than the Mausoleum and other Soviet-influenced structures, but its outward lines seem more spacious and inviting than its awkward and dimly lit internal spaces. The Museum also houses an extensive Ho Chi Minh archive (Logan, 1995a; Tai, 1995).

The Labour Cultural Palace

Another monument to Soviet architectural influence is the Labour Cultural Palace, originally known as the Soviet–Vietnamese Friendship Cultural Palace. The unimaginative, block-shaped edifice is all the more unfortunate in the context of the history of this important site, which has been described in some detail by William Logan and Soviet architects. It was here that the handsome headquarters of the 1902 Hanoi Exposition once stood, a Beaux Arts structure that later became the Maurice Long Museum. When Japanese forces occupied Hanoi in the early 1940s, these soldiers were billeted in the former exposition hall, and thus it was that American bombs destroyed the gracious old edifice during the

Second World War. 'Like other buildings constructed during the period 1955–90 when the former Soviet Union was Vietnam's main source of foreign aid and expertise', Logan writes dryly, 'its architecture owes little to the local culture' despite the use of some Vietnamese decorations and other minor elements. Logan continues more generally on a number of other undistinguished Soviet-style buildings:

Numerous new administrative buildings in Soviet versions of the Modern International style were built in the 1970s and 1980s and are marked by uninspired design, poor materials and, worse, disastrous siting decisions, having been unsympathetically constructed alongside, behind or in front of significant buildings of earlier times and architectural styles (Logan, 1995a).

The Hanoi People's Committee Building

The Hanoi People's Committee building constructed in a prime location along Hoan Kiem Lake, after a French colonial building was demolished, and connected awkwardly to other French structures, is an example of the Soviet modern international architectural style and the Soviet planners' 'great disdain for the French quarters, their villas and boulevards' (Logan, 1995).

*   *   *

These are but a few of what remain from an older Hanoi in the capital city. That they are interspersed with the buildings and areas of everyday life make these and other sites readily accessible to residents and visitors alike, history in the midst of daily life in a city where history and the vitality of a present-day capital merge with an effectiveness rare in today's Asia.

Appendix

Spring in the Royal City

Composed in 1508 by Nguyen Gian Thanh

The universe was created,
And the royal city was built.
Here gather mandarins in gorgeous dress,
Court music resound,
Culture and honor blossom.
The sky is filled with spring air, the whole universe gleams,
Like a solid pillar amidst the affluent nation stands the capital.

Since ancient times
We have been at the heart of the land.
At the summit of the country,
To the Southwest Tan mountain raises its peak to the roar of wild beasts,
To the Northeast, the dragon frolics in the waters of the Red River.
For a thousand miles stretch the hills and waters making ours a key position.
The four seasons are as many springs, when each one's flowers shine in all
     their brightness.
Everywhere proud edifices
And wondrous spots,
Nine-walled palaces of jade
Brightened by thousands of brocade robes
Everywhere, markets among the houses, like an immense fresco.
No end of busy quarters, where purple jostles vermilion.
Inside cavernous, austere palaces.
Golden doors bar the way.
Weeping willows waft like clouds,
Peaches in royal gardens redden like the cheeks of pretty girls.
The sound of flutes springing from a palace makes the moonlight tremble,
The drums in watch-towers urge the flowers to open.
The markets are more and more animated,
The streets rival one another in beauty,

Young men tuck up their tunics and play shuttlecock,
Blushing lasses arrange their breast-covers and trousers,
Noblemen on horseback admire flowers along the avenues,
Young people ride in carriages with open parasols, displaying their nobility,
What joy to be in an era of peace!
Tributes from every corner pour in,
The palace brightens up in spring
Men can now look forward to happy longevity,
From distant provinces carriages bring the people's homage
To a throne as unshakeable as the Thai Son mountain.
The nation, firmly installed on golden ground
Like the royal city, is blessed with abundance.
And indeed it is
A rich, wonderful royal city
Where spring shines in all its beauty
Can one dissociate spring colours form the splendour of the capital?
From the four corners of the compass everything converges on the heart
   of the land.
Every corner is a capital in miniature
However it is the city which makes the beautiful spring.
It is better to rely on human virtues than on advantages of terrain.
Many a country has built their power on citadels,
Let us rather make justice and humanity our fortresses,
So that generation after generation, spring after spring, our children may
   hand down our fine traditions for thousands of years.

(Translated and published in *Vietnamese Studies* No. 48 (1977); reprinted
by permission of the Foreign Languages Publishing House, Hanoi)

Bibliography

Anon. (1977a), 'Old Hanoi Evoked by a 19th Century Princess', *Vietnamese Studies*, 48: 163–7.

—— (1977b), 'Royal Edict on the Transfer of the Capital' [Thien do chieu], *Vietnamese Studies*, 48: 131–2.

Baron, Samuel (1752), *Description du royaume de Tonguin*, Paris; L'abbé Prevost.

Brookes, Graham (1994), 'Challenges for Conservation of Old Hanoi', *Australian ICOMOS Newsletter*, 14: 1, 5–6, quoted in Annalisa Koeman, 'The 36 Pho Phuong in the Face of Change', Hanoi, November 1994.

Dam Trong Phuong (1993), 'Conservation of the Valuable Heritage of Our Hanoi', Paper delivered at the opening ceremonies of the Friends of Hanoi Architectural Heritage Foundation, Hanoi.

Dampier, William (1931), *Voyages and Discoveries*, London: Argonaut Press.

Dang Thai Hoang (1980), *Ha Noi nghin nam xay dung* [Hanoi, Thousands of Years of Construction], Hanoi: Hanoi Publishing House.

Downs, Frederick (1991), *No Longer Enemies, Not Yet Friends: An American Soldier Returns to Vietnam*, New York: W. W. Norton.

Do Xuan Sang (1977), 'Hanoi's Old Quarter', *Vietnamese Studies*, 48: 168–72.

Duffy, Dan (ed.) (1996), *North Viet Nam Now: Fiction and Essays from Ha Noi*, Viet Nam Forum 15, New Haven: Yale University Council on Southeast Asian Studies.

Ennis, Thomas E. (1936), *French Policy and Developments in Indochina*, New York: Russell and Russell.

Garstin, Crosbie (1928), *The Voyage from London to Indochina: The Dragon and the Lotus*, London: William Heinemann.

Giang Quan (ed.) (1994), *Ha Noi trong ca dao ngan ngu* [Hanoi in Folksongs and Proverbs], Hanoi: Hanoi Publishing House.

Gillespie, John and Logan, William S. (1995), 'Heritage Planning in Hanoi', *Australian Planner*, 32 (2): 96–108.

Hanoi Culture and Information Bureau (1972), *Hanoi (Di tich va thanh canh)* [Hanoi (Traces and Landscapes)], Hanoi.

Hanoi muoi hai ngay ay [Hanoi, Those Twelve Days: Christmas Bombing, 1972], Hanoi: Literature Publishing House.

Hanoi People's Committee, *Regulations on Construction Management and Conservation of the Old Quarter of Hanoi*, 30 August 1993.

Hebrard, Ernest (1928), 'L'Urbanisme en Indochine', *Architecture*, XII (2): 33–48.

_____ (1932), 'L'Urbanisme en Indochine', in Jean Royer (ed.), *L'Urbanisme aux colonies et dans les pays tropicaux*, 2 vols., La Charite sur Loire: Delayance.

Hoa Bang (1977), 'The Temple of Literature and the National Academy', *Vietnamese Studies*, 48: 113–27.

Hoang Dao Thuy (1982), *Nguoi va canh Ha Noi* [People and Landscape of Hanoi], Hanoi: Hanoi Publishing House.

Hoang Huu Phe and Yukio Nishimura (1992), *The Historical Environment and Housing Conditions in the '36 old streets' Quarter of Hanoi*, Bangkok: Asian Institute of Technology.

Hoggard, Stuart (1993), 'Hanoi: A City at Risk', *Vietnam Today*, 2: 3, 31–7.

Ishtiaq Khan (1994), 'Safeguarding the Historic Quarters of Hanoi City', *Vietnamese Studies*, 42 (112): 128–32.

Johnson, Ian (1996), 'Decaying Homes were Once Hanoi's Pride: New Preservation Effort Attempts to Save Some of City's Old Charm', *Dallas Morning News*, 14 January.

Karr, Tim (1995), 'With Reconstruction Underway, Architects Hope to Preserve the Past', *Architectural Record*, July.

Le Thi (1995), 'How I came to the Vietnamese Revolution', in Duong Trung Quoc (ed.), *19–8 Cach mang la Sang tao: Hoi uc cua nhung chien si Viet minh trong Cach mang thang tam o Ha Noi*; forthcoming in *SIGNS: Journal of Women in Culture and Society*, 1998 (translated by Mark Sidel).

Lockhart, Greg and Lockhart, Monique (trans.) (1996), *The Light of the Capital: Three Modern Vietnamese Classics*, Kuala Lumpur: Oxford University Press.

Logan, William S. (1994), 'Hanoi Townscape: Symbolic Imagery in Vietnam's Capital', in M. Askew and William S. Logan (eds.), *Cultural Identity and Urban Change in Southeast Asia*, Melbourne: Deakin University Press.

_____ (1995a), 'Russians on the Red River: The Soviet Impact on Hanoi's Townscape, 1955–90', *Europe-Asia Studies*, 47: 443–68.

_____ (1995b), 'Heritage Planning in Post-doi moi Hanoi: The National and International Contributions', *APA Journal*, Summer, pp. 328–42.

Marini, J. P. de (1666), *Histoire naturelle et curieuse des royaumes du Tonguin et du Lao* [Natural and Curious History of the Kingdoms of Tonkin and Lao], Paris.

Marr, David G. (1971), *Vietnamese Anticolonialism, 1885–1925*, Berkeley: University of California Press.

—— (1981), *Vietnamese Tradition on Trial, 1920–1945*, Berkeley: University of California Press.

—— (1996), *Vietnam 1945: The Quest for Power*, Berkeley: University of California Press.

Masson, Andre (1929), *Hanoi pendant la periode heroique*, Paris: Librairie Orientaliste Paul Geuthner; portions published as *The Transformation of Hanoi, 1873–1888*, Madison: University of Wisconsin, 1983.

Matics, Kathleen I. (1994), 'Hanoi's Historic Heart: The Thirty-six Old Streets', *Asian Art & Culture*, 7 (Winter): 78–93.

Meyers, Dean (ed.) (1994), *The French in Indo-China With a Narrative of Garnier's Explorations in Cochin-China, Annam and Tonguin*, Edinburgh: T. Nelson and Sons; reprinted Bangkok: White Lotus, 1994.

Nguyen Bac (1994), *Giua thanh pho bi chiem* [In the Occupied City], Hanoi: Hanoi Publishing House; English translation forthcoming (Sidel, trans.), Cornell University Southeast Asian Program, 1998.

Nguyen Cong Tru (1977), 'Hanoi: Impressions', translated in *Vietnamese Studies*, 48: 162.

Nguyen Duy (1995), 'New Year's Fireworks', *Manoa: A Pacific Journal of International Writing*, 7 (2) (Winter): 94.

Nguyen Thanh Binh (1988), 'Nguyen Thanh Binh on Weaknesses in City Management', Hanoi Radio; 10 October; translated in British Broadcasting Corporation Summary of World Broadcasts (Far East, FE/0283/B/1, 15 October 1988.

Nguyen Thua Hy (1985), 'Socio-economic Features of Ancient Hanoi: 17th–19th Centuries', *Vietnamese Studies*, 6 (76): 87–101.

Nguyen Vinh Phuc (1979), *Duong pho Ha Noi* [Streets of Hanoi], Hanoi: Hanoi Publishing House.

—— (1981), *Ha Noi*, Hanoi: Cultural Publishing House.

—— (1995), *Hanoi Past and Present*, Hanoi: Gioi Publishers.

Pedelahore, Christian (1986), 'Constituent Elements of Hanoi City', *Vietnamese Studies*, 12 (82): 105–59.

—— (1993), 'Hanoi, Mirror of Indochine Architecture', *Vietnamese Studies*, 37 (107): 25–56.

Rhodes, Alexandre de (1651), *Histoire du royaume du Tunguin*, Lyon.

Robequain, Charles (1944), *The Economic Development of French Indo-China*, London: Oxford University Press.

Salisbury, Harrison (1967), *Behind the Lines—Hanoi*, New York: Harper & Row.

'Sedition in Tonkin' (editorial) (1907), *Straits Budget*, 17 January, in Thomas E. Ennis, *French Policy and Developments in Indochina*, New York: Russell and Russell, 1936.

Tai, Hue-Tam Ho (1995), 'Monumental Ambiguity: The State Commemoration of Ho Chi Minh', in K. W. Taylor and John K. Whitmore (eds.), *Essays into Vietnamese Pasts*, Ithaca: Cornell University Studies on Southeast Asia.

Tao Trang and The Hung (1977), 'Thang Long: The City and Its People', *Vietnamese Studies*, 48: 59.

The Hung (1977), 'Life in the Ancient City of Thang Long', *Vietnamese Studies*, 48: 60–144.

Thrift, Nigel and Forbes, Dean (1986), *The Price of War: Urbanization in Vietnam 1954–1985*, London: Allen and Unwin.

To Hoai (1973), *Chuyen cu Ha Noi* [Old Stories of Hanoi], Hanoi: Literature Publishing House; reprinted 1994.

_____ (1996), *Ha Noi va Ha Noi* [Hanoi and Hanoi], Hanoi: Hanoi Publishing House.

Tran Hung and Nguyen Quoc Thong (1995), *Thang Long— Ha Noi: Muoi the ky do thi hoa* [Thang Long—Hanoi: Ten Centuries of Urbanization], Hanoi: Construction Publishing House.

Tran Huy Lieu (ed.) (1960), *Lich su Thu do Ha-Noi* [History of the Capital Hanoi], Hanoi: History Publishing House.

Tran Quoc Vuong and Nguyen Vinh Long (1977a), 'Hanoi from Prehistory to the 19th Century', *Vietnamese Studies*, 48: 9–57.

_____ (1977b), 'Thang Long: The City and Its People', *Vietnamese Studies*, 48: 58–112.

Tran Quoc Vuong and Vu Tuan San (1975), *Ha Noi nghin xua* [Hanoi in Time Immemorial], Hanoi: Hanoi Publishing House.

Turley, William S. (1975), Urbanization in War: Hanoi, 1946–1973', *Pacific Affairs*, 48 (Fall): 370–97.

Van Cao (1995), 'Never Such Another Time', in Duong Trung Quoc (ed.), *19–8 Cach mang la Sang tao: Hoi uc cua nhung chien si Viet minh trong Cach mang thang tam o Ha Noi*, Hanoi: Vietnamese History Association.

Wright, Gwendolyn (1991), *The Politics of Design in French Colonial Urbanism*, Chicago: University of Chicago Press.

Index

References in brackets refer to Plate numbers; those in brackets and italics to Colour Plate numbers.